Love Letters
To My Brothers

INFINYT WIZDOM

This book is dedicated to all of the men in my life that inspired these letters. I'm hoping these words uplift and inspire you to be greater than you are today. For those that have passed on, I feel honored to have had you in my life. I love and miss you, and will never forget how you've helped me to become the woman I am today.

CONTENTS

I have a lot of experience with men. I've learned from my grandfather, my father, two stepdads, a father-in-law, four uncles, nine cousins, twenty-two brothers (including my seven brothers-in-law), my two sons, and, of course, my husband. They all love me and show me love, and over the years, they've taught me valuable lessons about life and men. They also know that I have high expectations of everyone around me, especially them.

I believe that men are responsible for taking care of their families and setting good examples for the younger generations. Not only financially but also as our leaders, teachers, protectors, comforters, confidants, supporters, and so much more. We not only learn this from stories in the Bible, but we've been taught this and have observed it in our own families. As a woman, I feel responsible in these very same ways to my loved ones. However, I definitely think men are supposed to add that extra guidance and security to our lives. In typing these words, it seems like a simple ask. However, that's not always the reality. Though I've seen great examples of this, such as my amazing grandfather and my beloved father-in-law, I've also seen many men struggle to maintain employment, be faithful to their wives, and be present for their children. Much less be able to be a financial provider. Some aren't even able to have a simple conversation with the women in their lives without being demeaning or disrespectful because of their insecurities and twisted concepts of male and female roles.

Don't get me wrong, I'm not saying that women are perfect. We all have baggage from our past and unresolved issues that we should be doing the work to address and correct. This work is necessary, so we won't continue to give these issues life by imposing them on others, especially those we should love. After seeing so much dysfunction and hearing how many men feel, I thought it wise to document some simple expectations. I chose to write these letters to you because some of the women in your lives feel that engaging in a conversation with you about many of these topics causes great stress. They are uncertain of how to share their concerns without hurting your feelings or being misunderstood. There's something about a conversation with your sister that's very different from a conversation with your mother or significant other. Your sister can communicate with you on a whole different level. There's a connection there, a bond, trust. We truly want what's best for you and typically don't want anything in return. We're not telling you what to do but instead calling things to your attention. I'm hoping that reading these words in the privacy and comfort of your own space makes it easier to understand and digest. The goal is to embrace wisdom and effect change.

With that in mind, I decided to write this book from a sister's perspective. It's a series of letters inspired by things I've experienced, witnessed, or heard about. I've shared some personal letters in a few of the chapters, as well, before getting into the expectations letters that I wrote for you all. So don't be alarmed when you start reading them. I'm not "Big Brother," and I am not proclaiming to know what's going on in your personal life. I am a big sister, though, and I know a lot of what's going on in the lives of the men around me, my family, and my friends.

I do believe there's something here for everyone, whether it's for you personally or someone you may know. You can take your time and read through each chapter in the order it is written, or you can bounce around and read the ones that are calling out to you first. I wrote it in an order that was meaningful to me, but it's yours. Take your time and work through it however you feel best. I just ask that you complete each chapter that you start, stay open-minded and read the entire book at some point. I truly believe that each chapter has something for you, whether it applies to your life now or in the future. If it's not for you directly, it might be for someone you may know. The point of this book is to wake up the brothers, who knowingly or unknowingly are holding our people back from having strong, healthy, productive families that breed generations of strong, healthy, productive children. So please, don't read it by yourself. Share it with a friend. Tell them to get a copy so that you can read it together. Talk through some of your feelings, whether you agree with me or not. Let's start some honest dialogue about these everyday issues and how we can improve our lives and those around us.

My hope is that once you have completed reading this book, you will no longer have to guess what women want from you or what your family expects of you. There's no judgment, accusations, or negativity associated with these asks, though I will sometimes be very direct. I'm writing from a place of love, hoping these simple changes can add more peace, love, and prosperity to your life and those around you. We all know that when you are living good and doing the right things, you can feel the blessings around you.

I'm not saying we don't have road bumps or challenges along the way. Those may simply be tests, and sometimes it's a smack in the back of your head to make sure you don't make a mistake. Stay in tune and be real with yourself. The point of the book is to show you some examples of things that may not have played out as they should have, how to correct them, see the fruits of your labor, and achieve your destiny. It's never too late. You always have the option to change your path. For some of us, it may require a little more work than for others, but it's still attainable. And why not? Why not make the changes necessary to be happier, healthier, and have more positive relationships? These changes can also lead to more love and maybe even more money in your pockets. So, why not?

Let's take this one step at a time and hopefully grow together as we read through these chapters and think about which of these things we need to consider in our lives. You may be doing some or all these things already. You may even be able to add to what I'm asking. If so, my contact information is at the end of the book. I would love to hear from you. Let's get started if you're ready to embark on this journey with me. I ask again that you read these words with an open mind and an open heart. Think about the life that you truly want and what you need to do to get it. Then ask yourself, why not? What's holding you back, and is it worth it?

Chapter 1: Accountability

"The steps of a good man are ordered by the Lord:
and he delighteth in his way."
Psalm 37:23 KJV

LOVE LETTERS TO MY BROTHERS

Hello My Brothers,

I'm glad you've decided to join me. It's time we have a long overdue talk. First, I want to thank the men out there that are handling their business not just in the public eye, where you can easily be deceived, but in their homes. The men that are truly doing the right things, where their families, the people who know what's really going on, can stand behind them and say, "Yes, this is a good one. He is a man of honor and integrity. He is hard working and does the right thing, even when no one is watching. He loves, respects, and worships the women in his life. He is a role model for the young men in the family. He doesn't try to act macho in the presence of other men, he simply does what's natural, and it's the right thing to do." I applaud you all and have a favor to ask. Spread your wisdom.

Encourage the men in your house, at work, at your gym, at your church, at the sports bar you hang out at, and every other man you encounter to step up and stop the nonsense. Encourage them to stop playing games as if tomorrow is promised, and they will always have a chance for a do-over. Call them out on their mess and challenge them to level up. Truthfully speaking, all the foolishness that most of them carry on doing is harmful to those around them. Their thoughtless, careless behavior is causing long-term damage to their loved ones and friends. And honestly, they're only able to do it because women allow it.

Because we love you so much, we sometimes offer you courtesies that you don't deserve. Sorry, but it's true. There are many times when we should tell you the straight truth, but instead, we sugarcoat it to spare your feelings or not bruise your ego. The problem is that the message then gets lost in translation. Since we weren't clear in our communication with you, you do not understand what's happening. You now think we missed it since you know what you did, and it wasn't called out directly, but you're mistaken. You're not slick and we're not naïve. Don't think that at all, or you'll be the one that ends up getting played. We simply are not firm enough to call you out on your bad behavior and hold you accountable for correcting it. The "whys" are different in every situation, but at the end of the day, it contributes to the same dysfunction. Our lack of consistency with holding you accountable and still expecting better and more is causing confusion, stress, and further disappointments and is ruining our families. Let me explain.

We, the women in your life, sometimes allow certain behaviors or are too easy to forgive when you haven't taken accountability for what you've done. You haven't acknowledged that you were wrong or provided some type of proof that you understood that your behavior was unacceptable, but we move on like everything's ok. We get so tired of fighting outside of the house, against all the forces that don't want to see us succeed, that we just want to be able to have peace in our homes. Our homes are our sanctuaries, and we don't want to fight or be on guard there. So, we pick and choose our battles. "Do I really feel like getting into it about this today? Will he even acknowledge my feelings or admit to being wrong?" The answer is usually no, and this is not a life-or-death matter, so we just leave it alone. Honestly, it's not always to avoid upsetting you, it's for our own peace and sanity, as well.

This unconditional love and lack of bandwidth for the drama has been mistaken for weakness, creating an environment where many of you feel you can do whatever you want and deal with the "consequence," which isn't much of a consequence at all. Sure, there may be a slight confrontation if we choose to address it and you don't acknowledge your "mistake" or our feelings. We may ignore you for a day or two if we feel frustrated, and then after a while, everyone goes back to business as usual. Forgive the comparison, but if this was what we did with our children, would they learn the lessons we were trying to teach them? Would they have a sense of right and wrong? Would there be any boundaries set? No! No! No! And that's what happens with you. And, let me just say that there are different degrees to this. Many may disagree, but I do not believe that all men are the same, so I'm not lumping you all into one category. The issues can vary from just not helping out with chores to being unfaithful in your marriage. In terms of accountability, that varies from person to person, too. Some men are very accountable and open to correcting their flaws, while others won't even engage in a conversation about any of their behavior that needs to be corrected.

What about a life in which you can wake up in the morning feeling good, get your day started, go to school, work, or wherever your destiny brings you and do it in peace? No need to try to figure out what to say or do. Just be you. Everyone is accepting you, just as you are. No need to lie or be fake. Handle your business, go home, and relax. Enjoy time with friends and family. How peaceful would that be?

Instead, many of you are hustling and juggling all types of nonsense throughout the day and not being productive. Then, you're stressed out at the end of the day because you really haven't accomplished any of your goals and still feel dissatisfied. What type of life is that? Why even continue to live that way? Then you have others who compare themselves to men who don't handle their business and say, "Well, at least I'm not doing that." You can't compare yourself to a zero and think it makes you a hero. If you want to compare yourself to anyone, compare up. Compare yourself to someone handling their business, then strive to match or do better. Don't patronize yourself by comparing downward. You're moving in the wrong direction, and your sights are already on the wrong goals. If you're having to trick yourself into thinking you're doing a good job, we really have some work to do.

Let me help you out with a few tips to effect change today. You can do simple things to be at peace and in good vibes with your friends, family, and, most importantly, yourself. Let me tell you what the women and children in your life are looking for. We want our men to have integrity, be accountable, show love more than ego, be compassionate, understanding, considerate, protectors, teachers, and leaders of our people. We want to be able to stand proudly next to you, knowing that no one can point fingers, whispering dreadful secrets that they think they know about you. We want to know that we can trust you to be in any environment and not get yourself into trouble because you're strong and cannot be tempted to do the wrong thing. We want you to be fighters, never giving up on your dreams or backing down from adversities. We do know that you'll get frustrated at times, but we want you to have good enough coping skills to communicate those frustrations in a productive manner and figure out how to get through. Yes, we want a lot, but you call yourselves Kings, so "heavy is the head that wears the crown." You are, as dictated in the Bible and tales from our ancestors, supposed to lead our people.

But how can you do that if you're not consistently doing the right thing and we can't trust you? We will not close our eyes and allow you to walk us off a cliff. We should be able to close our eyes and not be surprised when you walk us into our hopes and dreams, but unfortunately, so many of you have done just the opposite. So much damage has been done that many women believe it's impossible. They lump all of you together on some "men ain't shit" truck that's driving full steam ahead and expect the worse. Help me to change that perception. Show the world that you are powerful creatures that can accomplish anything you set your minds to. And these loving women I spoke about earlier that already show you unconditional love will be right by your side, being your partner and helping you to be successful. This is who we are and what we are about.

Now, I'll admit that a lot of us are not showing up like that anymore. The growing number of women that are now taking on the behaviors that we dislike when performed by men is astonishing. These women are so broken and tainted that they said, "Hey if we can't beat them, let's join them." This is scary, and it's a hot ass mess. We need to do something to correct this. You need to do something to correct this, and the time is now. So, let's get started and clean up the mess that you or your brothers have created, along with us women who were clearly ill-prepared to address this. We don't have a minute to spare.

Your Sister,
Wizdom

<u>Doing the Work</u>

Think about some of the requests you have received from the women in your life like your mother, sister, girlfriend/wife, or daughter. What are they asking you to do? Use the sections below to write down your thoughts.

Request#1:_____
Why have they made this request?_____
_____
How will it impact your life?_____
_____
How will it impact their life?_____
_____
Do you understand why they made the request and feel like it is reasonable? Yes or No.
If yes, what do you need to feel comfortable in following through with this request?_____
_____
Communicate this to your loved one and create a solid plan, with a timeline to get this done.
Plan:_____
_____
If not, communicate your concerns and see if you all can agree upon a plan that you believe to be reasonable, mutually beneficial, and will resolve the issue. Remember to be fair and treat people how you want to be treated.
Proposed Plan:_____
_____
Work through some of the other requests and even future requests in the same manner. Think about the life you want to live and how you can make it a reality. Keep doing your work, my brother. One step at a time.

Chapter 2: Dating

"...She may be weaker than you are, but she is your equal partner in God's gift of new life. Treat her as you should, so your prayers will not be hindered."
1 Peter 3:7 NLT

Please Read This Before Reading This Chapter
This chapter starts with a personal letter to someone who was not treating his girlfriend right. Then there is a second letter to all men that explains what women want from men when dating. It is not my intention to accuse all men of poor behavior. I know that all men do not cheat or mistreat their significant others. I would suggest you read the first letter, even if you don't feel it applies to you, because you may know someone that can benefit from hearing this message. The information in this chapter may help you to have a better understanding of how women feel in these situations and help you to have a conversation with your brother about doing better. Are you your brother's keeper? Yes, you are, and so am I.

Dear Brother,

I've watched your dating life over the years and have even seen you in "serious" relationships. In the beginning, you seem totally infatuated with these girls, almost like a prize you've been trying to win and ecstatic about finally accomplishing this victory. It's a beautiful thing to watch you try to impress these women, wining and dining them and wanting everyone to be on their best behavior when they're around. You really make us believe that they are the one.

Then some time passes, and I start to see little changes. As you get more comfortable, it almost appears that you start to slack off, which is a little shocking and disappointing because you've worked so hard to get into these relationships. Now it's starting to appear that you don't really want or value them anymore. Before you get offended or tell me that I don't know what I'm talking about, let me provide more details about what I've observed.

See, when you initially started dating, you couldn't take your eyes off her. It was as though no one else was in the room but the two of you. You would sit so close to her, embracing her as if you thought she would disappear if you let her go. Now, you're sitting a little further apart, on your phone doing who knows what. Don't let a pretty girl pass by because you are bound to peek and sometimes stare longer. What is that about? It's so disrespectful, and I know your girl sees you. They both do. Think of how embarrassing that is for another woman to know that you're with your girl but staring at her. Then you go from wanting to spend all your free time with your girl or at least being on the phone to now ghosting her and hanging out with the boys more. You don't want her doing this, though. You like when she's at home waiting for you, as you run the streets. And to be honest, because of the drastic change and assumed lack of interest in her, she can't really tell if you're just spending time with your boys or out with another woman. Her insecurities are heightened, and who can blame her? You're not communicating properly or behaving as you had at the beginning of the relationship.

This is not right. You have essentially tricked her into falling in love with your representative just to get what you wanted, which appears to be the right to say you had her. But now it seems you don't really care about how she's feeling. She clearly sees the difference. It's just a matter of time before she says something about it if she hasn't already. And what will your response be? How do you explain this abrupt change? Is it something that she did? Did you think she was one person, and she's shown you that she's someone else? Have you spoken to her about this? What's the deal?

Well, the whole family has fallen in love with her, because she truly is a nice girl, and we know that you are the problem. We've figured it out. You want your cake, and you want to eat it too, with no regard for how she feels. You still want to be with her and want the relationship you've established, but you want to go out and have "fun" with other people, as well. She can't do this because you wouldn't want your woman in the streets acting single. However, you expect her to accept this behavior from you. Did I sum it up correctly? Come on, dude. You know this doesn't make any sense.

Instead of you spending time and energy looking for someone to fill whatever gaps you feel your girl has, how about you have an adult conversation with her, expressing what you need in a respectful way? Maybe these are things she hasn't even considered and can actually provide. Maybe not, and you both can decide this is not the relationship for either of you. Whatever it is, close one book before opening another. Deal with the situation at hand, and don't drag someone else into the equation to skew the results.

I've also heard you talking about not being able to be with one woman and feeling trapped. This is just another aspect of the difference between men and women that I clearly don't understand. If you're in a healthy relationship, where you both have outlets and communicate your needs, why isn't one woman enough? Do you need space? Go and hang out with your friends and family. Do you want something out of the relationship that she's not providing? Let her know. Why does the answer have to be that you get it elsewhere?

Anyway, I have some expectations for dating and relationships that I wanted to share with you. These tips are based on events that I have experienced, witnessed, or was told about. It's nothing you haven't heard before, but maybe reading it will provide a little more clarity. You're a good man in so many other ways, but the cheating must stop. You really kill the trust in your relationship and cause unnecessary pain when you do this. If you were really interested in keeping your relationship, you would cut the mess and grow up. If she's not the one, let her go. You can't love someone so much but inflict so much pain and tear away at their confidence and self-worth. That's not love, my brother. It's a display of selfish, inconsiderate, mean-spirited behavior. You already know what's going to happen if or when she finds out. If you didn't want that outcome, why'd you do it? Time to take some responsibility for your behavior. Do better. Treat people like you want to be treated.

I still love you. That will never change. I just want you to do better.

Your Sister,
Wizdom

Dear Brothers,

When it comes to dating, there are some straightforward rules that can eliminate the stress and the drama. You see, dating is just what it says, dating. There is no real serious commitment until you establish that. If you are honest about your feelings and intentions, and you and the people you're dating are on the same page, there shouldn't be any issues. If you simply say, "I'm dating other people but would like to spend some time getting to know you, as well," then the young lady knows where she stands and can set realistic expectations around those rules. If you come back later and say, "I'm really enjoying our time together and want us to be exclusive," and she agrees, great. Now you cut everyone else off and let them know that you're in a serious relationship and can't see them anymore. It's all simple if you're honest with yourself and everyone else. If you stand your ground and follow through on what you said, no matter what the temptation is, you will be able to truly be faithful in your relationship.

The problems come in when you're dishonest, selfish, and playing with people's feelings. It could be because you can't make up your mind, or you're the jealous type and don't want the ladies you're dating to date other men, even though you're seeing other people, or you might even be afraid to hurt someone's feelings. Whatever the reason, once you start withholding information or straight out lying, this is when your problems begin. If you are honest with all parties involved, you are allowing them to make informed decisions about how they will interact with you going forward. If you are not, you're now misleading them, and when they find out, which you know they will, you create unnecessary problems, distrust, heartache, and drama.

Practice honesty. Don't make any excuses for why you did what you did. Just tell the truth. At least this will let the other person know that they can trust you. Whether they like what you're saying or not is another story, but you're letting them know where you stand.

And don't play the game of, "I don't know who to choose, but I want you to be monogamous with me." That's just selfish and ridiculous. Give your partner exactly what you're expecting them to give to you. If you can't decide, then continue to date until you can, and expect that these ladies will do the same. When you make up your mind, let them know. Hopefully, they're on the same page with you. You'd be surprised that neither one may be the right one for you. At least not right now, because if they were, you would know by now.

Don't feel like you have to rush into something serious, either. It is ok to just get to know people. The better you know them, the easier it'll be for you to decide if this is someone that you can be with for the rest of your life and trust to bear and raise your children. Ask yourself. If this is the woman that will help keep you on track and support you through thick and thin. It's not all about looks and popularity. That's on the surface stuff. You should be looking for your soulmate. Not saying she'll be perfect, but she will be perfect for you.

Make sure that you are presenting yourself in a desirable way, as well. Remember that while you are on your search for the right woman, these women are on the search for the right man. Good looks are going to get you in the room, but the rest of your package will determine whether or not you can stay. Sure, if you have a few bucks in your pocket, that may impress some, or you might just find a gold digger. Most young women are looking to see if you're motivated, have ambition, and have an actual plan to see your dreams through. They're asking themselves questions like, "Am I going to have to take care of this dude, or will we be able to take care of each other?" It's not only about fun for the moment, but actually how far the two of you can go together. Don't miss out on your "Mrs. Right" because you're out here playing and don't have yourself together. If you lose her, you won't be able to heal that wound easily. Stay focused on your business and career aspirations while you're dating. We'll talk more about dividing your time and focusing on priorities later. Just remember, she's testing you just as much as you are testing her.

So, date and take your time. Don't feel pressured to rush, and don't rush anyone else either. Be open and honest and give them as much space and time as they need. And when I say to date, I'm not saying you should be intimate with all these women. I'm more so speaking of spending time together and getting to know one another. Get to know your likes and dislikes and who your families are comprised of. Let her know if you have children or multiple women that you have children with. Anything she may find out later that can potentially be a deal breaker should come from you, early in the relationship, and before things get too serious. You don't want anyone else to tell her your story. Women hate when anyone else comes and tells them anything about their man. It's always easier to digest when it comes directly from you. Always remember that.

When you become intimate, you step into another realm of the relationship. Feelings will definitely be deeper on both sides. Then, in many cases, once you start having sex, it's an unspoken rule that you're taking the relationship to yet another level. Communication is very important here. If it is not your intention to actually have a deeper relationship with this person, be sure to state that before anything sexual transpires. This way, if she feels differently, she can decide not to have sex with you. Don't play games here just to get what you want because you may get more than you expected. Continue to tell the truth, no matter how much it hurts either of you, and takes things from there. And remember, no means no. This is the golden rule for men. It's pretty simple, no always means no. No matter what's going on or how far you've already gone, the minute you hear that two-letter word, pump your breaks, and disengage immediately. Don't assume she's playing games.

This is all about you being accountable and doing the right thing. Speak your truth and make sure your actions are aligned with your words. The responses you'll get from this level of honesty will be impacted by how the message is relayed. Don't be manipulative, speak with respect and consideration for the other person's feelings. You can initiate the conversation with a disclaimer: "I want to be respectful of your feelings, and I need to be honest with you, as well." Here you're placing the responsibility on them to receive it in the manner intended. Not saying things are going to work out as you'd like all the time, but as long as you put all of the cards on the table, you're playing a fair game. Relationships have changed so much over time. People are more open-minded nowadays. The key things that have never changed, though, are the need for honest communication and respect. If these two things are missing, true love is as well. Keep looking.

Don't settle because you're lonely or feel like time is ticking. Being in a healthy, fulfilling, loving relationship is too important. It's like you're baking a cake for your grandma. Instead of taking your time, following the directions, and making sure you have the best ingredients, you throw whatever you can find in a baking pan and give it to her even though it's not finished setting. No, thank you. She will not be accepting that mess. Take your time.

Don't waste time either by playing around and doing things that you know won't amount to anything. I'm not saying you can't have fun, you should be enjoying this time. We have one life to live, and tomorrow isn't promised to anyone, so we need to enjoy it, but we shouldn't waste it. I'm sure you know how to differentiate between spending time to see if she's the one and spending time just to pass the time. You'd be surprised by how fast you can blink, and years have passed. That's what causes all that undue stress and pressure to make things happen more quickly.

Another important thing when it comes to dating is truly being a gentleman and being considerate. As you're spending time with these lucky women, speak to them with respect and treat them with respect. If you ask them out, pay the bill. Don't suggest doing things that you can't afford to cover by yourself. And if they ask you out, if you cannot afford to go, make that clear and suggest something that you can afford, or see if she's ok with going dutch, where you both pay your own tab. She shouldn't be the one reaching in her purse unless she's treating you. This should be established before you go out, not while you're there because you just told her you don't have the money. Be honest about your finances so that there are realistic expectations, and she knows what to expect. It'll be really frustrating to both of you if there is no clarity about how money can and will be spent. There's nothing wrong with suggesting to stay in and watch a movie. Do what you can afford. If she's someone that wants more and is not willing to meet you where you are, and grow with you, maybe it'll be better to cut ties now.

Further, be mindful of their feelings and the things that are important to them. One thing men notoriously do is forget important dates or wait until the last minute to plan for events or get gifts. Don't be that guy. New Year's, Valentine's Day, birthdays, and anniversaries are important days for most women. Save the birthday, anniversary, and any other date that is important to her in your calendar on your phone or Google calendar with a recurring reminder. Be prepared to celebrate in a way that is meaningful to the two of you. This will let her know that she's important to you and that you care about how she feels. It really feels crappy when a man forgets our birthday or anniversary, and he has nothing planned or not even a gift to give us. It's as though we're not important or a priority.

And just forget about messing up on Valentine's Day if it's important to her. Listen, I get that everyone doesn't celebrate the same things. This is why we communicate about topics like this early in the relationship so that we can ensure both are the right fit for the other. However, if you do celebrate Valentine's Day and make plans to celebrate the day before or the day after, you'd better have a good reason. Why are you unavailable on the day of? This is the question your girlfriend will have, and you'd better have a good answer. She may assume that you are spending Valentine's Day with someone else, and that is not what you want. Society has coined the day before and after Valentine's Day as Side Chick Day, and this is not the title that she has assumed. Now, if you work and she knows you were at work and you all hang out afterward and plan to really celebrate on another day, then it's all good. However, if you're playing games, just know your cards are showing. This is why I say to be honest and let everyone know where they stand, then let them decide if they still want to participate.

Though you may be having fun, it's not always going to be fun times. There will be times when you have disagreements. Stick to the issue and don't bring up issues from the past. If you chose not to speak on it before, don't layer a new argument with it now. If tempers are too heated to have a constructive conversation, ask to finish the conversation later. Never say things to purposefully hurt her feelings because she won't forget them, and you may regret it. Never let things get out of control and become physical. You both should keep your hands to yourselves and refrain from doing anything that can cause the other harm. You both need to control your tempers and act like responsible adults. There are some things that we can't come back from. Know that. If she's the aggressor, walk away. When she calms down, you can first address the behavior that inhibited the necessary dialogue and advise her on how you would prefer to deal with conflict. Hopefully, she agrees because if she doesn't, you may just have to walk away. If you have been identified as the aggressor, you should get some help to correct this behavior. Figure out why you were triggered and why this was your response. Talk through some better ways you could have dealt with your feelings. We face conflict on a regular basis and must learn how to constructively maneuver through them. This is the only way you will develop healthy relationships in which you and your partner thrive. Isn't that the point to be happy, feel fulfilled, and enjoy life?

Remember, life is not a game. There are real rewards and consequences to your actions. People have feelings, and you can't simply say, "Sorry. I made a mistake. I didn't mean to hurt you." Not everyone will accept that. Treat people like you want to be treated. Be honest and communicate timely. Have good intentions for the people you decide to invest your time and energy into. And remember, if it's too hard, it may not be the right thing to do. Love has its battles, but shouldn't feel like a constant war.

I pray that you get to spend time with people that enrich your life. I pray that you have happy days filled with love and laughter. I pray that you find someone that motivates you and makes you feel safe and valuable. I pray that you find your soulmate. I truly believe that everyone has one, and I thank God for leading me to mine. Have fun and enjoy the journey.

Your Sister,
Wizdom

Doing the Work

I hope you enjoyed this chapter and possibly had a "light bulb moment." If you're not yet married and wish to be one day, I hope you're making the right choices to make that desire a reality.

Are you currently dating? Yes or No

If not, why?_____

If yes, are you dating anyone that has the characteristics you want your wife to have? Yes or No

If not, why are you still dating this person? Do they have the potential and want to meet your expectations? _____

If she does have those characteristics, are you in a monogamous relationship with this person? Yes or No

If yes, great. I hope she has the same feelings about you. Keep building a strong bond and making plans for your future together.

If not, why not? What do you need in order to commit to a monogamous relationship? Make sure she knows how you feel and the two of you are on the same page and working towards a mutual goal._____

_____

Are you being honest with the women you are dating? Yes or No

If so, great. Keep speaking and living your truth and remember to treat people like you want to be treated.

If not, why do you feel like you can't be honest? What do you think is going to happen if you tell the truth? Do you think you'll have a better result now or when she finds out that you've been being dishonest? _____

_____

Take a deep breath and let out the truth. You can do it. You will be ok.

Chapter 3: From Boy to Man

"When I was a child, I spoke as a child, I understood as a child, I thought as a child; but when I became a man, I put away childish things."
1 Corinthians 13:11 NKJV

Please Read This Before Reading This Chapter
This chapter starts with a personal letter to someone that is young but has a lot of responsibility and is not adjusting well. As with the previous chapter, this chapter has two letters. The second letter is directed to all men. However, the first is still a good read. It gives a very good example of the struggles some men face with maturing and handling their business. The person in the first letter has a family, and whether or not you have one, it still speaks to growing up and being responsible for taking care of yourself and your responsibilities. It also gives a little clarity to why I felt it was necessary to discuss the expected changes from boy to man. Enjoy!

Dear Brother,

I've seen you struggling over the past few years with managing your responsibilities and dealing with the consequences of not really handling your business. I've tried to give you the right advice, I want you to get on track, and I don't want you to lose your family. You guys are beautiful together, and your kids need you. I'm not really sure how to help anymore, though. I've talked about the things you can do to show that you're being more responsible and what needs to be done to stabilize your family. I know that you know what to do and can actually do it because I've seen you do it. The problem is consistency. You'll do good for a while and then just fall off. What's going on? What causes you to lose sight of your responsibility and goals?

I can't in good conscience continue to speak on your behalf if you are not willing to consistently do the right thing. I don't want to feel like I'm helping you to mislead anyone and to be honest, I understand why she's fed up. You're a grown man with children. You live with them and their mom. This means that you can't sit home playing video games all day. You must participate in taking care of your kids and maintaining the household for your family. You can't say that because their mom works and can afford to pay the bills that you don't have to contribute. This is a responsibility that you should share, especially because she is telling you that she's overwhelmed. Why should her money be used to handle business while you spend yours however you see fit? How is this fair or appropriate? Then you want to throw a tantrum and act out when you're addressed. That may get her to leave you alone temporarily, but it doesn't solve the problem.

Your kids are watching you, bro. You are teaching your son how a man is to behave. You are not setting a good example. You are showing your daughter how men will treat her. Is this what you want for her? It couldn't be.

Look, I know you've faced some disappointments in your life, and unfortunately, a lot of people have. You must learn from your experiences, adjust, and continue to try to thrive. You can't just give up. You need to be able to take care of yourself and your children. No one is responsible for taking care of you at this point. You're an adult. You have to grow up and start acting like one. You need a place to live, so you need a job that can pay your rent, utilities, grocery bill, car note, and insurance. If the one job you have isn't enough, get a part-time job. You have children that require parenting. Work with your girl to decide who will be responsible for what and get it done. These things are not optional. They are your responsibility.

You can't expect that your relationship will work when your woman is constantly stretched, stressed, and disappointed with you. You can't keep allowing things to get so bad that she wants to leave, then you play on her emotions and try to make her feel sorry for you, so she won't go. Get help if you're having issues. Figure out what you need to do to be able to overcome some of your obstacles. Don't just completely spiral out of control, then beg for forgiveness and start doing right long enough to gain her forgiveness, and then start the vicious cycle all over again. No one is going to stay on this roller coaster with you indefinitely. You're lucky she's stayed this long. She has to do what's best for her and her children. Your behavior is now being viewed as manipulative because you don't follow through on what's necessary to ensure you don't get to this low place again. You do just enough for the moment, and then it's back to losing focus on handling your business and taking care of your responsibilities.

I'll say it again. Stop focusing on what you want from her in a relationship and just focus on getting yourself together and taking care of your kids. This should be your priority right now. Once you have that in order and you're consistently doing what you need to do, then you can focus on your relationship. You need to get counseling, get your finances in order, solidify housing, and get back on your feet. Focus on you. Everything else will fall into place when it's supposed to. I know there's love there, but there's also so much hurt and disappointment that there's no room for a healthy relationship to flourish right now.

I'm praying for you and will be here to support you. Focus and be disciplined. No more wasting time and money. No more temper tantrums. It's time you display the behavior of a healthy, determined, disciplined, considerate, grown man. You are not a kid anymore. You actually have kids of your own that need you to behave like a responsible dad. I know you didn't experience one, so you should be trying harder to give your kids a different experience. Break the curse. Don't allow another generation to suffer the same dysfunction you had to. Everyone's counting on you and rooting for you. The time is now. Get it done.

Your Sister,
Wizdom

Dear Brothers,

I have to say, the biggest complaint I get from most of the women I speak with is the lack of maturity of their partner. There's always a statement of frustration that's followed by, "He really needs to grow up. I'm not his mother. I'm not raising a grown man, l have my own children that I need to raise…." The causes of these statements vary. It may be that the guy won't get a job. Or, if he does have one, either he's irresponsible with his money and can't properly contribute to his responsibilities, or he doesn't make enough and won't seek an alternative or supplemental job. When it's not the finances, it's his lack of support. He's not helping with responsibilities, like chores, or the kids. Another may be the fact that he'd rather sit around playing video games in his spare time than entertaining his partner. Whatever it is, these behaviors are unattractive to women.

You're not going to look the same, display the same behaviors, or have the same responsibilities when you're 30 years old as you did when you were 16. Time has passed, and with that, you should be wiser and more mature. You should carry yourself differently, as you have a better understanding of your situation, what is socially required of you, and how you want to be perceived. Again, there are cultural differences that may impact how this looks, but the key to it all is continuous growth. It should include progress that makes you more prepared and accountable for handling your business. Let's get into it.

If you're a young man and you don't have any children yet, your life is a little simpler. You have more time to figure out what you want to do and who you want to be. You can follow a pretty basic structure. For those under 25 years of age, you're most likely in school or getting some type of training to prepare you for your career goals. Depending on your resources, either your parents are still supporting you, or you may have a job to cover your living expenses. Hopefully, you've been advised well and trying to save money. You're just starting out and should be building your credit, not messing it up. This will play a huge part in what you're able to do for yourself and your family later on in life. So, pay your bills on time. If you can't afford something, it's not wise to buy it. At least, not right now. Be patient and disciplined. Be careful and live within your means. Don't use money and material items to impress people, then get yourself into financial trouble. You don't have to do that for your real friends, and everyone else can kick rocks. Still, hopefully, you're living the life of your dreams and enjoying it to the fullest. Hanging out with your friends in your free time while you all motivate each other to get to this bag the legal way. You should also be looking for the woman of your dreams if you haven't found her already.

A few years from now, you'll be at the age or point where you may be starting your career and settling down in a relationship. You may even be starting your family. Here's where things start to change, as you have to be more mature and start to really consider how your behaviors impact others. You'll have more bills and really need to know how to balance your checking account to ensure that your bills are covered and that you have a little change left to enjoy life. You'll have a more defined schedule, as you'll have a job, need time to work out, and also allocate time to spend with your special lady and other family and friends. You might feel like your circle of friends get smaller or starts to change. As you get older, people will move in different directions and have different interests from you. You may even change your style of dress to separate yourself from the younger crowd. This is not to say you're no longer "young and fresh." You're just taking your style up a notch, as you know more about fashion and have more money to get nicer things.

Be careful not to overindulge. Prioritize needs from wants. For example, you may want to get yourself an affordable car that you're proud of. This comes with other expenses like insurance, gas, and maintenance. Make sure you are making enough money to cover these expenses, as well as rent, utilities, groceries, your student loans, and any other bills you may have. A responsible man, which is who you are striving to be, handles his own finances. Make this your priority. Financial stability will impact you for the rest of your life. Falling short in this area will negatively impact other areas of your life and contribute to your stress. Get it together. No excuses. If you can't find one job to cover your expenses, think about getting a part-time job until you can get the credentials you need to get a promotion or cut back on some of your expenses to balance things out until you are able to take on more. Either way, just be responsible. This is important to your parents and any woman you are pursuing. They all need to know that you'll be able to take care of yourself independently. They'll all be proud of you, and you will feel proud and accomplished, as well. Think back to all the achievements you've had that have put smiles on the faces of your loved ones. This can be from little league championships to graduations, to the random times when you've done the right thing, and they shook their heads saying, "Yes. He gets it, and his behavior shows it." How did it make you feel? Good, right? That's the feeling you want to continue to have. A sense of accomplishment. Being able to have pride in knowing you are doing the right thing and handling your business.

Managing your health is important now too. Your parents may have been scheduling your doctor's appointments when you were younger, but they shouldn't be anymore. Make sure you have a primary care physician that you see annually for a physical. Preventative care is better than getting sick and being reactive. Go to the dentist every six months for a cleaning and any other work you may need to be done. Your mouth is an important part of your overall health. Having an infection that you're unaware of can cause serious health problems. To cover some of these expenses, you'll need medical and dental insurance. You get these great benefits from that full-time job you're holding down and thriving in. If not, you'll have to have some way to buy into a personal plan, which can be very expensive, or you can get public healthcare, if possible. I would suggest that you get a job or some form of business where you can have the money or benefits to take care of yourself.

Now when you're over 35, you move into a more grown and sexier zone. No one wants to see your boxers anymore, so no more sagging. Pull up your pants. At this point, you may be more established and growing in your career. Marriage and children may be factors in your life that have really elevated your level of responsibility. You may have moved from paying rent to having your own mortgage, and the expenses have really kicked up. You may be working, married, and raising your family, so time is of the essence, and you need to be really organized so that you can take care of yourself, as well.

How are you feeling? I know it can all be a little overwhelming, but if you've been slowly working towards these things, you shouldn't feel so much pressure. The key is to enjoy life and all of your accomplishments. Don't look at your added responsibilities as burdens but rather accomplishments and take on the responsibility of taking care of them with pride. You are a grown man with grown man responsibilities. Make your parents proud. Heck, make yourself proud. Balance your time and money so that you can take care of yourself and the responsibilities you've gained along the way. The last chapter in this book, "Taking Care of Yourself," gives a lot of details about managing your time and taking care of yourself. Skip ahead and check it out if you want, but mark your book, so that you don't miss anything here.

In terms of managing your money, Oprah presented a great debt diet that I often refer to. I have found this to be extremely useful and manageable if you are disciplined. You can find it on her website, Oprah.com, but here's a sneak peek.

- ❖ 35% of your income goes to housing: mortgage/rent, repairs, taxes, utilities, insurance
- ❖ 25% to other living expenses: eating out, vacations, entertainment, clothing
- ❖ 15% to debt: student loans, credit cards, personal loans
- ❖ 15% to transportation: car payments, gas, insurance, repairs, tolls, train/bus fees
- ❖ 10% to savings

She didn't go in-depth in terms of your savings, but the point is to save 10% of your income. You can put it into a savings account, establish a 401k, get a Roth IRA, and so much more. You can reach out to a financial adviser for more guidance. The point is to establish some type of savings for retirement and any unexpected expenses that may arise. It's not a matter of if but when, so make this a priority so that you're not in a bind when you have a need. And if you have the money, you should also create separate savings for your children to help them to start their lives after high school. Whether it be for college or a business venture, they'll be so grateful.

Now here's the fun part. When you are 45 years of age and over, it's time to start planning for that retirement. Retirement is the time in life when you can work if you want to but won't have to. This could be a time when your mortgage, car notes, and student loans are paid off, your children are grown and on their own, and the only expenses you have are your basic utilities, groceries, prescriptions, gas, and whatever perks you want to enjoy. We're not there yet, but this is what you're planning for now.

Hopefully, you have an established 401k, stocks, and some other investments in play. If not, get this done, if possible. The more passive sources of income you have, the better. Your career may be approaching its peak if it's not there already. You should feel comfortable in your craft and stable in your career and finances. You and your beautiful wife may be able to start traveling, if that's your desire, and enjoying life more. You may have to help your parents out a little, depending on their health and financial status, but this is really your time and your family's time. You and your wife get to relive the honeymoon years. I'm hoping you've kept the fire burning, but now it's time to crank it up again. You've worked hard to get to this point where you're truly enjoying the fruits of your labor. It'll get better once you retire, but don't wait until then. Get the party started now. You don't have to overdo it, but let's get back to date nights and cranking up the romance at home, as well. You may not be in that infamous "empty nester" stage yet, but you also may not have little ones that are totally dependent on you anymore either. Attend your kids' activities and plan family vacations. Use your free time to enjoy life and create memories.

Then when you retire, the world is yours. This age varies for everyone, based on how well prepared you are. And again, it may not mean that you've completely stopped working. You've hopefully been blessed to start or continue doing what you are passionate about and leaving your legacy. You should be on your own schedule and running your own show. This is my wish for you. I just hope it's your wish for yourself, and you have the discipline, wisdom, and strength to see it through. You do not want to be lonely and live in your parent's basement for the rest of your life. They don't want that for you, either. They want you to meet your soulmate and have a successful life. One that you are proud of. One in which you feel blessed and fulfilled. Make it happen, my brother.

Your Sister,
Wizdom

Doing the Work

Let's talk about how you want your future to unfold.

- ❖ What are your goals and aspirations for your career? What type of training or experience do you need to accomplish this? How long will it take, and when can you start?
- ❖ What is your credit score? What do you need to do to improve it?
- ❖ Use Oprah's debt diet to see how much money you currently have to contribute towards each group of expenses. Are you currently over budget in any area(s)? If so, I challenge you to make the necessary adjustments to balance your budget and live within your current means. It may hurt a little now, but trust me, it'll definitely pay off later on.
- ❖ Do you plan on getting married? If so, to whom and by when?
- ❖ Do you want to have children? If so, how many? When do you want to have your first? Where will you live?
- ❖ What age are you looking to retire? What's the plan to ensure that becomes your reality? Do you have a 401K that you are actively investing in? If so, how much money will you be able to have monthly, based on your current investment? Will it be enough to cover your expenses? Do you need to be saving more? Do you have other savings, stocks, or other investments to supplement your income?

Think about these questions for a moment and start to develop your plan. It may not manifest exactly as you desire, but at least give yourself a framework by which to function. Let's make it happen, bro. Fill in the blanks below.

Right now, I am going to_____

In 1 yr_____

In 5 yrs_____

Chapter 4: Being a Good Husband

"For husbands, this means love your wives, just as Christ loved the church.
He gave up his life for her."
Ephesians 5:25 NLT

Please Read This Before Reading This Chapter
This chapter starts with a personal letter to my husband. There is a second
letter that follows, in which I share expectations for all men who have been
blessed with the title of being someone's husband. Though I'm mainly
speaking to married men, I would suggest that single men read it to get a
better understanding of what women expect from you once they become
your wives. Consider it a little study guide to help prepare you before you
take that big step into marriage.

31

To My Beloved Husband,

When you asked me to marry you, I was overjoyed. I loved you so much and you asking me to be your wife showed me that you loved me deeply, as well, and wanted to spend the rest of your life with me.

This made me feel even more responsible for taking care of you, supporting you, helping you to accomplish all of your goals, and making sure you were happy and satisfied with me. You were my friend, my high school sweetheart, and the love of my life, and I wanted to be the best wife possible. I wanted to ensure that you knew you made the right decision in picking me for your wife. I just knew that you would take care of me with the same energy.

31 years have passed since we've shared love and 20 years since we've said, "I do!" A lot has transpired in that time, including the birth of our three beautiful children and me gaining a wonderful stepdaughter. I've had moments where I was overjoyed and moments where I truly questioned whether we would see another year together. Though I've faced some disappointments, I've also experienced a lot of joy, and I'm still here, still loving you, still attracted to you, still wanting to be your wife, and still wanting our happily ever after. I know that you are my soulmate, and we are stronger together. As we continue to grow as individuals, we will grow as a couple, learning to be better people and spouses.

If you don't know by now, you have my heart, and there is no one that I would rather be with than you. I'm standing by your side, through thick and thin. This doesn't mean that I'm not going to communicate about concerns or issues as they arise. It just means that I am willing to work through our issues to resolve them and ensure they don't repeat themselves. I have high expectations and will continue to push you to be better every day, not just as my husband but as a man of God, Mrs. Julie's son, our children's father, and my friend. I know who you are and what you're capable of, and I want the best of you and for you consistently. Blessed is the man that does better because he knows better.

This is one of the most important relationships I have ever had, and it has taught me a lot about myself and life. Maintaining a happy, healthy marriage takes work. I'm going to share some of what I've learned that a man needs to bring to the table. I hope that you will agree and be proud when you read this. Love you now & always.

Wizdom

Dear Brothers,

I pray that you find a beautiful wife. A woman that puts a smile on your face and makes your heart flutter when you see her. A woman with dignity and integrity that loves you and worships the ground you walk on. Someone that will love you unconditionally and be your rock when you're in need. You want a woman that has nurturing qualities, that will take great care of you and your children, whether she gave birth to them or not. A woman that knows how to cook, and I mean really knows how to cook and keep a clean home. A woman that your mother loves and trusts to take care of you. An intelligent, independent woman that can be a great housewife or a successful businesswoman. A woman that's strong enough to have difficult conversations with you when needed and wise enough to know when to back off and let you lead. A woman that is pleasing to you in every way.

I also pray that you behave in a manner that makes her feel you are deserving of such love. I pray that she can trust you to always do the right thing by her and your children, never putting yourself and your needs above that of the family. When you take a woman as your wife, you gain a life partner and the responsibility of taking care of her and the children that she bears. The words "taking care of" have a broad meaning, so let's be specific.

Physically, you are to be their protector. A loving security guard would be a good analogy. Do your best to make sure they face no harm from you or anyone else. This means you have self-control, keep your hands to yourself, and you're present and available to assist, as needed, from any other forms of harm or danger.

There will be times when you and your wife disagree. This is normal. The way you handle it, though, is very important. Please let cooler heads prevail. Saying hurtful things or putting your hands on your wife are absolute negatives. Don't do it. Words cut deep, and physical contact of any kind will never be forgotten and can lead to more trouble than you ever imagined with your wife and the law. Domestic violence must not be an issue in your home.

Let me say this goes for both people. As the man, if you see the argument escalating out of control, end the conversation and revisit when both of you have had time to cool down and think about how you want to proceed. If she doesn't stop, it's better to walk away than engage. If she becomes physically aggressive, restrain her in the safest way possible, ask her to calm down, and walk away when you can. Striking her back or restraining her in a way that can cause physical harm can lead to trouble. The last thing you want is to have the police in your house and a domestic violence case on your record. Be smart. I know it can be hard in the moment but be in control of your emotions. And later, when you have the opportunity, communicate your expectation that she keeps her hands to herself, just as she wants you to. Remind her that you have a crazy sister. Just kidding. But seriously, physical violence is unacceptable. Get some help if this is an issue.

On a lighter note, I know that everyone needs their downtime to hang out with friends and get a break from their daily responsibilities and unwind. Do this in moderation. Make sure you've taken care of your responsibilities at work and home and that your wife is ok with you stepping out. I don't want you to think of it as asking for permission, though, but rather you are checking in with her to make sure she's good too. You don't want to make any assumptions about how her day has been and whether she needs your support or not. You play a vital role in the development of your children and supporting your wife and kids. They need you to be present and engaged. In the same breath, staying home but locked away in your "man cave" is not good either. Be a part of the team. Help get things done so that everyone can get a chance to chill and relax before starting all over again the next day.

Another aspect of being a good husband is being romantic and loving. Greet your wife with a hug and kiss all of the time, even if you're not getting along. Ask how she's doing and if there is anything that you can do for her. Make sure she feels like you're her man and not just someone she's sharing responsibilities with. Wine and dine her, just as you did when you were trying to convince her that you were the one. You should do more now as a sign of appreciation for her committing herself to you. Be a gentleman. Open her doors. Take her out on dates, to places that she actually likes, and not the bar that you meet your boys at. Make time for her. Compromise and don't think everything has to be about you or go your way. Fix things when they're broken before she has to ask for the third time. Cut the grass and take out the trash. Keep her car clean and gas tank full and handle the maintenance. Celebrate her milestones and successes. You should be her biggest and most supportive fan because you should be more concerned with her happiness than anyone else's.

Nowadays, men are looking for women to do all of this for them and calling themselves kings. This is very similar to the role confusion of those that sit back and watch their wives pay the bills when they are able-bodied and capable. This is not right and not the behavior of a decent man. If you're calling yourself a king, who is your queen, and how does she deserve to be treated?

This brings me to another topic that's important to men and can be equally important to women, sex. Make love to your wife on a regular basis, and make sure she enjoys it. Sex drives are different for everyone. So, talk about it and come to a happy compromise for frequency and all other aspects of the process so that you both will be pleased. Don't get caught up on who initiates. Just make love to your wife. And remember, it's not a race that you want to win. We all know you'll more than likely achieve your climax before it's all said and done. Make sure she does too. This, for sure, is not the time to be selfish. Take care of your wife. Trust me, if you give, you'll get a lot more in return. That's just how we're built.

In terms of finances, make sure your wife has a place to call home, with utilities working and food to cook to put on the table. This means you need to stay employed and manage your finances appropriately. Pay the bills in your home before spending anywhere else. You cannot take care of others if your home is lacking. And we all like nice things. However, it is your primary responsibility to ensure that these bills are paid first before splurging on anything else. Issues in this department may lead to your wife having to step up and be the main financial contributor, which means she won't be as available to take care of the house, kids, or you. Now, if this is what the both of you agree upon, and it works for your family, fine. Just know that it now means that you have to help with these other things: the house, the kids, and her. It's not ok to want your wife to do it all. She is going to be stressed out and resentful, and a lot of things are going to fall through the cracks. This won't only affect you but your children, who won't get the time and attention that they need. Step up and pull your weight. Don't let immaturity, ego, arrogance, or any other controllable factors influence the decisions surrounding you taking care of your primary business, your family.

Save and plan for your financial freedom. You cannot spend every penny that you make, or you will never be able to retire. Yes, I know we want to enjoy some of those fruits of our labor now because tomorrow isn't promised. I get it. But if you eat all of the fruits now, you won't have any for later, and a hungry older person is not a good look. You do not want to be a burden on your children. Sit with your wife and come up with a budget that will cover your current expenses, allow you some freedoms to enjoy some perks, and save for the future. You both need to be on the same page when it comes to the finances of the house, or there will be strain and disappointment somewhere and cause unnecessary strife.

Pray with your wife. Thank God for all of the blessings He's given you and ask Him to forgive you for your sins and guide your behavior so that you're worthy of more blessings. Ask Him to guide your lives so that you think, speak, and behave like a good man and husband, and she like a good woman and wife. Ask Him for protection against the enemy and his plan to tempt you and lead you astray. Ask for wisdom so that you can lead yourself and your family in the right direction. Ask for the right words and actions to get the job done. Then thank Him again for having provided you with another day and another opportunity to make Him proud.

Be a good role model for your wife and children and encourage them to always do the right thing. Teach them right from wrong. Acknowledge good behavior and discourage negative behavior. If you read the Bible, there is clear guidance on behavior that is pleasing to God and will lead to your salvation. Encourage this and teach your children to be strong, loving people that will be able to take great care of your grandchildren. Help to steer their lives in the right direction so that they become loving, responsible, productive members of society that you can be proud of.

Support your wife in parenting your children. Don't argue with her in their presence. Arguing in front of children causes so much harm and anxiety. Not only may they feel they are to blame, but it also puts them in a position to have to take a side, which is harmful to the child-parent relationship. Also, don't disregard your wife's rules with the children. If she requests something of them, back her up. Don't ever allow them to do the opposite. This rendition of "good cop, bad cop" will cause further issues and give the perception that they don't have to listen to her, as she is not an authority figure. If you disagree with her decisions, speak about it privately and make a joint decision about how to move forward. If there is a change of heart, allow her to share it with the child. Don't ever allow for the perception that you are overriding their mom. This will set the stage for her being disrespected later. And all these rules apply to your wife, as well. Hold her accountable to the same standards and speak about it privately if there is ever an issue.

Treat your wife like you want to be treated, and don't take her for granted. Communicate about your concerns in a productive way and work together to resolve them. If she has shortcomings, don't just give up on her and find a replacement or supplement. Just as you wouldn't want your wife to go out and find someone to fill in all the gaps you have, in terms of checking off all her boxes, give her the same grace and show her the same respect. She's not your girlfriend. She's your wife. Your time for figuring out who you wanted to be with passed when you asked her to marry you, and she accepted. Don't be fooled or tempted by another because she appears to be what you want or need at that moment. Especially if you have already complained to her about all the things that upset or disappointed you about your wife. You have now given the other woman the playbook to win you over, for the moment anyway. This is very important because infidelity ruins trust, which can ruin relationships. If you thought you had issues before, they will only get worse once you betray your wife in this way. No matter how much she tries, as you display behavior that causes the smallest bit of concern, there will be issues. This type of betrayal causes a wound that will never completely heal. It may appear to be closed, but the slightest touch will reopen it again. And please don't just assume that she won't find out unless you plan on doing your dirt on another planet. Even then, someone will see you get on that spaceship.

Be mindful of how you talk to people about your wife, especially when you're angry. We sometimes communicate what was done to us rather than telling the whole story so that the listener can fully understand what transpired. This is not only unfair to your wife but may change people's perception of who she is and, hence, their behavior towards her. Though you may have just been venting and may not have meant everything you said, you are shaping an image of your wife that will stick. They are not going to forget what you told them. Even when you've worked through this issue with your wife and moved on, the person you vented to may still harbor negative feelings. This is especially true for your female friends and family members, who are overprotective and won't truly hold you accountable for your behavior but would highlight your wife's. Brother, the last thing you want is for the women in your life to be at odds. Trust me, it'll be a bigger headache for you than anyone else. Having your mother and wife, or sisters and wife engaged in strife puts you in a position to take a side with the most important women in your life, and they all expect your support.

My suggestion, talk to God. He actually knows what transpired and will guide your heart to do the right thing. This can be through prayer or even journaling. I know, I know, most people do not like to write their feelings down, mostly for fear of someone else reading them one day, but you would be surprised by how therapeutic this is. And honestly, if someone is rude enough to read your personal thoughts, whatever they read is on them. You do not owe them an explanation. You were upset and venting your feelings in order to appropriately process and resolve an issue. You needed that moment to get that stuff off your chest and have the right to do so. Writing it down, for your eyes only, is better than using these words in an argument with them or in a negative conversation about them. That could be very ugly. At least this way, it was between you and God, and you protected her privacy and feelings. Now she needs to respect yours. Additionally, if this helped you to properly organize your thoughts, you have already communicated your feelings in an appropriate manner, and you both have resolved the issue. This is water under the bridge. No need to revisit the issue. Anyway, just to be safe, you can destroy the entry once you're complete if your privacy is a concern. The point is to have a safe place to vent and process your feelings, rather than being hurtful to your wife directly in an argument or passively in communicating about her negativity to others.

Support your wife with her goals. Motivate her and help her in any way possible. Let her know that you want her to be successful in areas, even outside of being your wife and mother to your children. Know that she may need other outlets, just as you do. Don't concern yourself with whether she'll be more successful than you or be so insecure that you don't want her to be outside of the home, possibly interacting with the opposite sex. Have enough trust in and respect for your wife to know that she will not disrespect you or herself. And anyway, this is not about you. This is about her, and she has the right to set personal goals for herself. She doesn't completely lose her identity when she becomes your wife. And you all are not in competition. You are a team, working together to ensure that both of you are fulfilled and working towards your individual and family goals. Just because she may not "need" you financially doesn't mean she doesn't need you physically, emotionally, spiritually, or in any other way.

In every aspect discussed thus far, communicating honestly, openly, and respectfully will be essential to the success of your marriage. If you're vulnerable with anyone, it should be your wife. This is the person that is most impacted by anything that you do, so she should be the person that you share your secrets with, get advice from, and plan with. She is your partner. If you can't communicate with her in this manner, there's a problem, and it needs to be discussed. You shouldn't lay in bed with someone every night, eat the food that they cook, entrust them to care for your children and your household, but not trust or respect her enough to have serious conversations with her. And I don't mean coming home rambling about your day in a superficial way. I'm talking about, "Hey babe. I have something I've been thinking about, and I want to run it by you to see what you think." Or even, "I'm trying to accept what happened, but I'm really still struggling with XYZ." Talk to her. Especially if she can tell that something is bothering you and asks if you're ok. Don't just say yes and keep being awkward, looking miserable, not communicating, staying out all day, drinking more, and crashing as soon as you come home. Since you don't know how to or don't want to communicate with her about what's clearly bothering you, you're shutting her out, and believe me, she feels it. So, because you won't communicate with her about what's really going on, she's left to try to figure it out on her own, and the last thing you want is for her to be "making up a story" and acting on it because you won't communicate the facts.

This all comes down to you not respecting your wife as your partner but rather your roommate, housekeeper, babysitter, or someone to have sex with when you're horny. We are much more than that, and men that are wise enough to know and embrace this tend to live happier lives. They have a friend and life partner, someone to take some of the burdens off them. They have someone that they can truly be themselves around. They have someone that they trust to tell them the truth and not judge them. They have someone that loves and supports them, and they know it and act on it. This is how you should feel about your wife, the woman you asked to spend the rest of her life with you.

Trust is a huge factor in relationships, especially in a marriage. Withholding information is just another form of deceit. When you are doing things that you can't tell your spouse, you know it's wrong. Don't do it. If something does happen, tell her. Don't avoid the issue until you have to deal with it because, during that delay, more fuel is being poured on the fire. Now she's questioning why you withheld the information for so long and what else you are not telling her. Don't open the atmosphere to assumptions and unnecessary drama when you can clear the air immediately and move on. Figure out what's inside of you that is causing this behavior and address it before it causes you problems.

These are the behaviors of a strong, confident, loving, considerate, respectful married man. You are not single anymore and cannot expect to function like your single friends. Get yourself some married friends and encourage each other to do the right thing. Don't allow egos and the need to appear macho to prevail. Act like a "good man." Have self-respect, discipline, morals, and values that others desire to have. Be a leader and encourage others to lead their families in a peaceful, happy, healthy, productive lifestyle.

I'm praying that God opened your mind and your heart so that you have received this message as intended. Not only to benefit others but to benefit you and aid you in having a long, healthy, peaceful, loving, prosperous life. Remember, I want you to be happy, and ensuring your wife's happiness will bring you that if she's the right one. As they say, "happy spouse, happy house." Get to work, Bro. Good luck.

Your Sister,
Wizdom

Doing the Work

Think about the expectations that were expressed in this chapter.

❖ What areas are you excelling in?

_____

Thank you! Give yourself a pat on the back and keep up the good work.

❖ Which areas can you improve in? List them out in order of greatest to least impact and get to work. Identify specific steps that you need to take to make a change for the better. You can even speak to your wife about it and allow her to be your accountability partner. If this relationship is important to you, you want to show up as your best self every day. Just as you would if it was your dream job, and you were trying to impress your boss.

1. Area Needing Improvement:_____
   Plan:_____
   Step 1: _____ Completion Date: _____
   Step 2: _____ Completion Date: _____
   Step 3: _____ Completion Date: _____
2. Area Needing Improvement: _____
   Plan: _____
   Step 1: _____ Completion Date: _____
   Step 2: _____ Completion Date: _____
   Step 3: _____ Completion Date: _____
3. Area Needing Improvement: _____
   Plan: _____
   Step 1: _____ Completion Date: _____
   Step 2: _____ Completion Date: _____
   Step 3: _____ Completion Date: _____
   (Do this for each area you would like to improve in. Don't try to do too much at once. We're focusing on quality, not quantity.)

Chapter 5: Being a Good Father

"Start children off on the way they should go, and even when they are old,
they will not turn from it."
Proverbs 22:6 NIV

Please Read This Before Reading This Chapter
This chapter starts with a personal letter to my father. There is a second
letter that follows that applies to all men. I would recommend you read the
first letter to gain some perspective, even if you don't feel it applies to you.
There are several lessons in the first letter that I'm hoping will hit home,
such as, "It's never too late to right your wrongs." Enjoy!

Dear Daddy,

Though we've had many conversations about our relationship and our feelings, I believe this is the first letter I've written to you. Let me start it off by saying, "I love and appreciate you." Once upon a time, you loved my mom, and the two of you got together and created me through love. I hope I've made you proud.

You know that I always keep it real, so let's get to it. We all know that you could have done a better job with parenting, not only me but all of your twenty-seven children. Documenting the count is significant because it gives some basis for your absence. There's no way that one person can reasonably and responsibly be accountable to seventeen women and twenty-seven children. You've admitted that you were lost and didn't really know the magnitude of the hurt and pain you were causing. You've even apologized to many of the women and your children, as many of us have been able to ask the "whys" and communicate our feelings about our perception of our upbringing. I appreciate being able to have those conversations with you. I appreciate that you love and respect me enough to treat me like your adult daughter. That's why I always say, "It's never too late."

When you came back into my life at the age of twenty-six, just as I was about to marry the love of my life, that was a turning point for both of us. Though my stepfather walked me down the aisle, you were right there waiting in the aisle after I said my vows and took that first walk with my husband. I needed you at that moment. Right there, to support me and celebrate this new chapter. This was the first time that I can remember you being there to celebrate a significant milestone in my life. Thank you! From that moment on, I've truly felt your presence as my dad. You've remained consistent, and we've been there to support each other, as father and daughter should.

Though most of your children are grown with children of their own now, you still have some work to do, by repairing some of the damage that has shaped our lives. Many of us still have some healing to do, and it won't happen without some one-on-one conversations and sincere accountability. I know some may say it doesn't matter anymore and people are grown, but as we know, hurt people hurt people. Addressing some of the feelings of abandonment, neglect, and even unworthiness can have such a great impact on how we live the rest of our lives and treat other people. Please don't miss this opportunity to right some of your wrongs and help

45

your children to be whole and feel worthy so that they know how to express love and empathy for others. In addition to how they should be treated by others, particularly your daughters. I'm not saying that they won't know these things if you don't talk to them, because some of us have good coping skills and had others to step in and provide what you were unable to. I'm just saying it will make a difference coming from you.

I can say that I am so grateful to have you as my dad. I've expressed to you before how I had loving stepfathers that made me feel loved and cared for, in addition to my grandfather and uncles. I'm also happy that you were able to meet my father-in-law, who is basically responsible for many of the expectations that I have. To these men, you owe a great debt because they have been consistent and available to my siblings and me, helping to shape us into the adults we are. They were a part of the village, an important part. I know that you know that, and I love how appreciative, respectful, loving, and humble you are with them. That shows a lot of character on your part. You are a special man, sir. You've made some mistakes, but I acknowledge and appreciate that you're trying to redeem yourself.

You know I can go on and on, so I'll end it here. I love you, and I hope that you are once again proud of your "baby girl" once you read this book. Talk to you soon.

Your Daughter,
Wizdom

Dear Brothers,

I mentioned earlier how my father-in-law shaped many of my ideas of what a good dad looked like. Unfortunately, he has since passed, but the impact he had on me and so many others is everlasting. Pa, you were truly the best, and I dedicate this section of the book to you.

Just to clarify, there were other men that helped to raise me, like my grandfather, stepdads, and uncles. They helped to frame a lot of my impression of who a dad is. However, I spent so much time with my in-laws when I was a teenager that my father-in-law's presence, unconditional love, patience, understanding, and "everything is ok... nothing is a problem" attitude really had a huge impact on me. He had ten children, and he made time for all of them and me. He made sure everyone felt loved and special. He drove a yellow cab in Manhattan and brought home a pocket full of money that he handed to my mother-in-law every night. He trusted her to do the right thing with it, and she did. He brought home a bag of snacks, as well. Always having something for everyone, including me. He was just the sweetest, most considerate, loving man I had ever experienced. I had never seen anything like that before or after him. He was an amazing man, and I miss him dearly.

As you know, fatherhood is a very significant role. Whether you are married to the mother or not, your responsibility to your child does not change. You are to be present, engaged, and actively participating in your child's life, every step of the way. From ensuring that your child has a stable roof over their heads, food to eat, and clothing on their backs, to make sure their homework is done, and they are being good students, to making sure they have good manners, discipline, and appropriate behavior. You are responsible for teaching them about safety and defending themselves. You are responsible for keeping them safe from harm. You are supposed to teach them how to ride their first bike and drive their first car. You're also supposed to find out what their talents are and what they love to do, and help them to explore these things, whether it's sports or the fine arts. Never impose your will on them. Don't try to live through your child but find out what it is that they love and help them to flourish in that area.

You are to be present for every milestone, whether it's a birthday, school play, graduation, prom, and definitely their wedding. You are to be there every step of the way, grooming them, ensuring they become a good person and productive member of society, and most importantly, making sure they feel loved and supported. If you make a commitment to your child and tell them that you are going to do something, be sure to follow through. Don't tell them you are on your way and never show up. Don't tell them you are buying them something, then don't buy it. Be honest with your children and follow through on your promises. If something comes up and you are unable to follow through, communicate this timely, with a plan to correct it. Do not disappoint your children. Sometimes it's better to surprise them than to tell them you will do something and not do it. All these things contribute to their impression of you and will impact your relationship.

Remember, they are watching you. You are teaching your daughters how men are to behave and how they will treat them. You are teaching your sons how they are to behave. Be mindful of how you are with their mom, how you are with them, and how they perceive you as a person. I can almost guarantee that you will see patterns in their lives based on what you have taught them, consciously or subconsciously. I have brothers that weren't even raised by my dad and act just like him. They, my brothers that is, say it's in their DNA. Who knows? What I do know is that they've heard so many stories about him, both good and bad, and have felt his absence. Similarly, my dad's father wasn't in his life, just as he wasn't there for many of his children, either. As we know better, let's do better and break the curse. We can stop this dysfunction if we want to.

Be your child's biggest cheerleader. Don't compare your children to other people or show favoritism amongst them. Love all your children the same and let them know how special they are as an individual. Don't take sides in their arguments but be neutral and help them to resolve it, if possible. Never ask one to minimize themselves for the benefit of the other. Teach them how to teach people how to treat them, not only by their words but by their actions. If you see them behaving in an inappropriate way, address it. If you feel like something is not right with them, be there to support them and help them to correct it.

As they get older, treat them as adults, and not as children, even though they are your children. Loosen the reigns and allow them to fly. They will make mistakes. Simply be there to support them. You don't have to clean up their messes for them, either. Give advice, if requested, and let them grow from their experiences. Teach them a sense of responsibility and accountability. Take care of your children, and help them to be healthy, confident, loving, productive people with good problem-solving skills and coping skills.

That's it. That's your job as a dad. Doesn't seem that difficult, right? Unfortunately, many children don't have this experience. Some don't even know who their fathers are. Now, this isn't always the man's fault. However, from the time you become aware of your child, I hold you responsible for making these things a reality. I don't care how difficult the relationship with their mother may be or what legal hoops you have to jump through. You are responsible for managing your responsibilities to your child. If you didn't have a good relationship with your dad, make it up by having a great relationship with your child. Break the curse. Show them what a phenomenal dad looks like. Make sure your child never feels the things that hurt you as a child. And don't stop once they're grown and have their own children. Stick around and be the best grandfather possible. Support your child in being a good parent. We all know that it's probably the most critical, tasking job in the world for a man. Help your children to give their children the best experience possible.

This is a huge responsibility, but don't think that you'll be expected to do it alone. I'll be here, along with everyone else that loves and supports you, because we do know that it takes a village to raise a child. The bigger and stronger that village is, the better it will be for your child. But don't get carried away and try to pawn off your responsibilities on others because then you'll run out of favors. Support and taking on your responsibilities are two totally different things. Your village is here to support you. Call upon us when you need a hand, not when you don't feel like being bothered. We're all counting on you to do the right thing.

Your Sister,
Wizdom

Doing the Work

Think about your relationship with your child(ren). If you have more than one, think about each one individually.

- ❖ Are you proud of these relationships?
- ❖ Is there anything that you wish was better?
- ❖ Do you spend enough time with them?
- ❖ Are you financially supporting them?
- ❖ Do you know what they are interested in? How do you support these interests?
- ❖ Are they having any struggles? Behavioral? Educational? Physical? How are you helping to improve or resolve these issues?

I challenge you to talk to your child(ren) with an open mind and heart and ask them if there was one thing that you could do better, what would it be? Be very careful and listen and not provide a rebuttal or excuse to their answer. If this is mishandled, you may lose their trust and not get another opportunity to have this conversation. Simply listen to their response and develop a plan together to ensure you meet their needs going forward.

Now, here's a bigger challenge. Have a conversation with your child's mother. That's right! Ask her if there is anything that she feels you can improve upon when it comes to fathering your child(ren). Give her the same level of attention, grace, and respect that you gave your child. No rebuttals or excuses. Work with her to develop a plan to address her concern. Commit to the plan and follow up to ensure she sees the progress, as well.

Remember, this is all about you providing your child(ren) with the best experience possible. If you're capable, why not? Let's set our children up for success. There will be plenty of disappointments in life. You don't have to be one of them.

Chapter 6: Being a Good Son

"Hear, my son, your father's instruction, and forsake not your mother's teaching, for they are a graceful garland for your head and pendants for your neck."
Proverb 1:8-9 ESV

Please Read This Before Reading This Chapter
This chapter starts with a personal letter to my two sons. They are 15 and 27 years old. The first letter speaks to how a mom feels about her sons and her desires for them. The second letter, which is to the general public, speaks to the expectations of mothers from their adult sons. I would suggest you read both, as the first refers to the type of relationship our family has, hence the level of expectations. I say that only because I know that all families function differently. Nonetheless, I also know that we should treat people how we want to be treated, not necessarily how they've treated us. This is your opportunity to show your mother how much you love her and appreciate her for giving you life.

To My Baby Boys,

I know you're not babies anymore, but you'll always be my babies. No matter how grown you get and how deep your voices are, every time I look at you, I see my sweet baby boys. I am so proud of you both and truly enjoy watching you grow into powerful, respectable men. I get compliments all the time about how sweet and well-mannered you both are. I watch how people just gravitate towards you, as they admire you and want to be in your presence. This is a testament to your character, so don't ever change. Just continue to grow stronger, wiser, and more patient.

I know we live in a want everything, get everything right now type of society, but take your time and make good decisions. We are blessed, and God always provides us with what we need when we need it. I know you both have big, ambitious dreams, and I pray that you accomplish all that your heart desires. I just want you to know that it may not be on your timing, and you're going to have to work for it. You are both fighters, and I know you won't ever give up because of a little adversity. I want you to expect it and have the wisdom and determination to push through it. Don't ever let anyone or anything discourage you. Keep fighting for what you want, always. People miss their blessings by quitting at the very last minute and don't even know it. We are here, me, daddy, your sisters, and the rest of your village, to support you and see you through.

Don't let "life" control your time. You control your time. Know what's important and dedicate time and effort to these things. Keep yourself on a schedule if you need to, and designate time for the things that are important to you. You'll have school, basketball, work, family, friends, relationships, social media, and various other entities pulling you in different directions. Don't allow this to overwhelm you. You must learn to say no to some things and no to some people and that's ok. This is your one life to live, and you need to live it true to yourself, beliefs, goals, and dreams. This is how you'll find true happiness.

Also, everyone will always have opinions on what you should be doing, usually based on their life experiences. Listen, but always do what it is that your heart is leading you to. See, the beautiful thing is that everyone has their own life to live. We will all be responsible for our own decisions, so we need to follow our own paths. I'm not telling you not to take guidance. I'm telling you to listen and embrace the things that ring true to your heart. Those talking to you mean well and don't want you to make the same mistakes they did and truly believe that they know what's best. It just may not be what's best for you. Stay in control of your own destiny. No one stops your show but you. Do the right things, and you will be led in the right direction.

That's why you pray and talk to God. He's all-knowing and will never lead you astray. Talk to Him daily. Thank Him for all the blessings He's provided to you. Ask Him to guide and protect you. Then thank Him again, in advance, for seeing you through. He will never leave your side, and you should never forget to contact Him daily, several times per day if you need to. Pray and be conscious enough to know when and what He is communicating to you. To do this, you must give yourself quiet time to think, meditate, and reflect on what's going on around you.

I know that was a lot to digest. Fortunately, you'll have these words to read over and over, as much as you would like. Please read all the other chapters, as well. Mommy has some advice for you on how to flourish in happy, healthy relationships. Day by day, you'll see, hear, and experience things that shape how you view the world and, eventually, how you live. I'm sharing with the world some of my ideas on how men can improve their lives and relationships and possibly impact those around them. I hope you learn a lot and that you're inspired to influence others to be better.

Love you,
Your Mom & Biggest Fan
Wizdom

Dear Brothers,

When we talk about being good sons, some may think that this only applies to the youth, but it doesn't. As a son, you can have an impact on your parents if they are alive. Of course, when you're younger, your relationship and responsibilities to your parents are different, but the overall concept of how you should treat your parents is generally the same.

Treat your parents with love and respect and have a little patience with us. Yes, you're older now and free to make your own decisions. We can't tell you what to do anymore, but it doesn't mean you shouldn't listen to our advice. As parents, we are still going to try to protect you. It's hard to turn off that parent switch, especially for helicopter moms like myself. Yes, I've heard that so much that I've just decided to own it and wear that crown proudly.

I trust my kids to make the right decisions, but if I feel like they're about to make a mistake, it's difficult not to intervene to try to protect them. Of course, as you get older, we are supposed to let go of the reigns and allow you to make and learn from your mistakes, but trust me, it's not that easy. It's hard for parents to see their children in trouble. Be patient with us. Don't take on the attitude of, "I'm grown and don't need your help... don't tell me how to live my life." Even though this may be true, be gentle with us. Hear us out since you know our intentions are good. You may agree with some of what's being said, and you may not. Just have the conversation, then thank us for caring and let us know that you'll tell us if you need help. That's a polite way to say, "Thank you, but no thank you."

It's a fact that we're not always going to be on the same page. In fact, the older you get, the more we'll probably start to disagree. Know that we are trying to guide you in the right direction and protect you. That's all. The advice simply gives you more tools to utilize when necessary. And don't worry, the hovering won't last forever. It's a process; the older you get, the more we'll let go. And please don't think that it's because we don't trust your judgment. This is more about us than it is about you. We're so accustomed to taking care of you and making all the decisions that it just takes a little while to let go.

The tables are turning, and the older you get, the more we'll probably need assistance from you. Being patient and understanding is just the beginning. We may need you to take us to medical appointments, pick up our medications, take out the trash, and fix things around the house as they break. Or do other little things that will help us to continue to thrive at home and feel safe and secure. Cut your dad's hair and beard or take him to the barbershop. Take me to the salon to get my hair done. And we both can enjoy manicures and pedicures together. You can even join us. Your presence will mean a lot, especially as we start to need more and more assistance. Hopefully, this won't feel like a burden, though. Hopefully, you'll see it more like adult chores and things you do as a contributing member of a healthy family. If you get to a point where it feels like too much, please speak up and seek help from other family members or professionals as needed. We do not want to be a burden on you.

As you take on some of these responsibilities, be mindful though of respecting our wishes and desires. Don't try to take total control over everything unless you feel like we're starting to have some cognitive issues. In that case, please get us some help and do the best you can to start managing our business. Hopefully, we'll have our living wills and powers of attorney in place to help guide you. And even more so, hopefully, none of this will be necessary. In speaking with my grandmother, who's 91 years of age, I know that it is important for elderly people to maintain some control over their lives. She admits to needing assistance with certain things. Still, she gets very frustrated when she's treated as if she's incapable of caring for herself or her husband and not given options for managing their affairs. Though my mom, aunt and uncles may have good intentions, their actions ruffle her feathers sometimes. So, remember, we are still your parents, not your children. This is not your time to take over and give the orders. Follow our lead and be there to support us as needed.

Visit frequently, and bring the grandkids, especially on holidays. Most older people like company. Their lifestyles may not be as active as they used to be, as they may not be working anymore and aren't able to get around to visiting with friends much. Try to fit them into your schedule and spend time with them. If your parents enjoy spending time with the children, ask how frequently they would like their company and try your best to accommodate. Even with my parents, I can tell that they love to have my siblings and their grandchildren around, especially those that are retired and don't have much to do at home. They enjoy our company. However, keep a pulse check to know when they need a break. Over time, you'll learn the appropriate cadence.

I hope that, as you get older, you get to know your parents on a deeper emotional level. I pray that your relationship continues to flourish and that you understand and appreciate each other more. Your parents were responsible for protecting you when you were younger, but that ball will shift into your court as you get older. Take care of your parents, make sure they have everything they need to thrive, and make sure that no one takes advantage of them. Unfortunately, some people prey on the elderly, and because they may be lonely, they become easy prey. Keep a watchful eye and make sure this doesn't happen. They're counting on you.

Your Sister,
Wizdom

Doing the Work

As we discussed in the previous chapter, the older you and your parents get, the more you should be having conversations about their needs and wants. If you have not done so already, ask your parents a few questions. Also, spend time observing on your own, as some people are very proud and will not ask for assistance. Based on your findings, offer assistance where it's needed. Be sure to find out:

❖ Is there a living will or power of attorney? Discuss where they are located and what it entails. (Remember, this is not for you to question or challenge. You are collecting information so that you will know what to do if and when you need to.)

❖ Are there chores around the house that you can offer some assistance with? Whether you do it on your own or enlist someone else to, what things are they finding more difficult to complete independently?

❖ Is there anything they would like to do outside of the home? Where and when? Do they want to participate, or would they just like for someone to do it?

❖ Are their meds on mail order, or do they have to be picked up from the pharmacy? Would they like it to be mail ordered?

❖ How are they getting to and from their appointments? Would they like company when they go? I would suggest posting a calendar on the refrigerator and advising them to list all their appointments. This way, when you and your siblings visit, you can check to see what's coming up in the next week and devise a plan to assist as needed.

Communication amongst all active participants will be very important. Firstly, we want to make sure your parents have the support that they need and want. Secondly, no one needs to be overwhelmed. Share the responsibility to make things easier on everyone.

Chapter 7: Being a Good Brother

"… Am I my brother's keeper."
Genesis 4:9 KJV

Please Read This Before Reading This Chapter
This chapter starts with a personal letter to my biological brothers. You may share some of their traits, and you may not. Though they have similarities, they are all very different men. The second letter, which is to the general public, speaks to the expectations sisters have of their brothers. As in earlier chapters, I would suggest that you read both. I don't want you to miss a thing.

My Sweet Brothers,

How I love you all so much. As we've grown older and live in different places, I value the time we share more and more. I get so excited when I see you, as expressed by the big smile and never-ending hugs. I love spending time with you, not only because you make me feel so special, but because I have these moments to reminisce on the times that have passed and now reflect on how grown and handsome you have become. I'm so proud to be your sister. Thank you for giving me so many things to brag about.

Before I go further, I must clarify that when I'm talking about my brothers, I'm not only talking about the ones given to me by my mom and dad but also by my aunts and uncles. By definition, you all are my cousins, but in this family, we were all raised like brothers and sisters. We are all siblings in my book.

The love I have for you all is hard to describe because it is very similar to that of my sons but different, as well. From the time we were younger until now, I've always felt the need to protect you. No matter how old you are, the lioness is in full effect, helping to protect her coalition. I pray for you all the time, as I know the dangers lurking daily for our young men. Then you add in the lifestyle that some of you choose to live, which further increases my anxiety and stress. As I get older, I try to pray more and stress less, but it's not easy.

I've talked as openly and as bluntly as I could with you all about life and the decisions we make. Fortunately, and unfortunately, we've seen people thrive, and we've seen them fall. Though the sensible thing is for us to learn from the mistakes of our elders, we sometimes somehow fall right into the same path, with the belief that we're smarter and more prepared to handle the things that they fell short in.

As your sister, all I can do is be here to support you. I love you so much and see your potential and wish that I could dictate your steps, from choosing women to careers to health choices and everything else, but that's not how real-life works. We all have our own hearts and minds and make our own decisions. In my mind, my job is to try to influence and encourage you to make the right decisions, not only for you but for my nieces and nephews, whom I love so dearly.

I also have expectations of you in terms of how you treat me and the other people in our life, particularly the women. Throughout this book, you can hear my perspective as you read the relevant chapters. In this chapter, though, I'll address your direct relationship with me and your other sisters. Yes, as much as we are here to support you, we do require support too. In case you don't know what that looks like, I'm going to share it.

I hope you listen with an open mind and heart, and though some of you may already be perfecting some of these things, others need a total mind shift. For example, your man code cannot apply to the women in our family. You cannot treat us like you treat other women. We deserve a more sacred position in your life and to be treated with more respect and regard than you would someone that you know more casually. We are your family, the women that have your back, no matter what, and we give you unconditional love. We want the same.

You can see where I'm going with this, so before I spill all the beans right here, I'm going to close your letter and start the conversation with everyone. You know I'm tough, but you also know that I love you to death and will always be here for you. You might have to hear my mouth for a second, but in the end, I'm always going to support you.

Your Sis & "Ride or Die"
Wizdom

Dear Brothers,

I hope that you feel a certain responsibility to protect your sisters, not only from strangers but from anyone. I say this because as much as we love for you to like the men that we bring around and get along with them to the point where you could become "boys," we don't want you to become so close to them that you value that relationship more than the one you have with us. The men that we introduce into the family should not feel that they can behave differently in your presence than they would in ours. They shouldn't feel like they can approach other women in your presence, and you would be ok with this. If they happen to make this mistake, we expect you to address it. Now I'm not saying to be aggressive and violent. I'm simply saying to pull them to the side and be very clear that you are not going to allow them to disrespect us. Of course, every man does what they want, so we're not expecting you to be able to stop whatever they are doing. We just expect you to check them and put us on. Yes, that's exactly right, do for us what you would want us to do for you.

If a man we are dating shows you who they really are, you should make sure we know who we are dealing with. Now, it's our decision to stay in this relationship or not. You're not telling us to break up with him, just relaying what you know. We should also respect our relationship enough not to immediately run back and repeat what was said. I mean, we'll decide how this will play out. A man should never feel like you are ok with him violating your sister. He should also have enough respect for you to not violate us in your presence. Know that if you allow this and turn a blind eye, it's just the start of more to come, and we can get hurt in the end. We can experience a hurt that you could have prevented.

In line with this, give us the example of how a man should treat us by displaying this in your relationship with us and others. Make sure we know that men are to treat us like queens and make us feel special. He is to never embarrass us or intentionally hurt our feelings, and he definitely shouldn't put his hands on us. Talk to us openly about these things and make sure we have the type of relationship in which we can talk to you about anything. This means you have to earn and keep our trust and make sure we know that you have our backs.

Don't be afraid to call us out when needed, either. You should be the first one to gently pull us by our shirt tails and nicely check us about how we look, how we're behaving, and who we're spending time with, male or female. This is the part of taking care of each other and the responsibilities we have to one another. It's not to say that we'll immediately listen, but trust that we hear you. Even if you don't see an immediate change, your words definitely mean something, and we will consider what you've said. If there is any one man that should be able to have a brutally honest conversation with us, it's you. Dads and boyfriends or husbands will have the burden of worrying about our feelings a little more than our brothers. Our brothers can shoot it straight. If you do it privately and come from a good place, we shouldn't expect anything else. Even if we get into our feelings and tell you to mind your business, remind us that we are your business, and you're not trying to be mean, controlling, or hurtful by just speaking your truth. After that, your job is done, and it'll be our decision on how to move forward.

As we get older, stay in touch, and make sure we are doing well. Be there for our children if we have any, especially if their dads aren't in the picture. Kids love when their uncles are around. I know mine do, and I'm the same with my uncles. It makes our village feel bigger and lets us know that we have that much more support. Remember, your nieces and nephews look up to you too, so be a good role model. Don't let them see you doing things that you wouldn't want them to do. No matter what you say, they may follow your lead. That old saying, "do as I say, not as I do," doesn't work. Everything they see us do they feel is like a rite of passage. They just can't wait to do it one day. Be mindful of this.

That's it. I know you have your own life to live, and your hands are full, so I don't require much. Just be a good brother and another good example of the role a man plays in a woman's life and with her family. I'm counting on you to handle your business. Get a good job so that you can take care of yourself, deal with your emotions properly, so you can stay out of trouble, and find a strong, beautiful, nurturing wife to bare me amazing nieces and nephews. I'll let you decide on how many because you need to be able to properly take care of them. Just help to continue our bloodline with strong, healthy, intelligent, honest, compassionate, productive people. I'll be a good auntie and be there to support you all. I promise.

Your Sister,
Wizdom

Doing the Work

Do you feel like you have a good relationship with your sisters? Can they trust you? Do they feel protected by you? If any of this is in question, what can you do to correct it? List who you want to resolve an issue with, the issue, your plan of correction, and the deadline for addressing it.

Who? _____

What? _____

How? _____

When? _____

Are there any conversations you've needed to have with your sister(s)? What has held you back from having it? Are you afraid to hurt her feelings or concerned about how she will respond? If so, be clear with her about this when initiating the conversation. "I've wanted to talk about something with you for some time, but I don't know how to say this without possibly hurting your feelings or upsetting you. It's important to me to talk with you about this, though, so I'm asking your permission now." Here you've made her aware of your concerns and the urgency to have the conversation. Hopefully, you have her full attention, and she's braced herself for what's to come. Be delicate but be honest. Make sure she knows that you have her best interest at heart, and this is the only reason you've put yourself out there.

Who? _____

What? _____

How? _____

When? (Setting timelines helps you get stuff done.) _____

Chapter 8: Being a Good Friend

"My command is this: Love each other as I have loved you. Greater love has no one than this: to lay down one's life for one's friends."
John 15:12-13 NIV

Dear Brothers,

I have honestly never had a real male friend as a teenager or adult. I mean, I grew up in neighborhoods that had boys that we hung out with, but once I became a teenager, I wouldn't say they were my friends. It seemed like as we got older, most of the boys that were friendly wanted to be more than friends. I met my husband when I was 14 years old. We would talk and hang out in groups of teenagers, and we weren't initially interested in one another. Over time (4 months to be exact), those feelings quickly changed. We genuinely got to know one another on a strictly platonic basis and realized that we really liked each other more than friends. It wasn't just about appearances or reputations but a genuine connection.

I find the same happens with most of my sisters. Typically, when they are hanging out with males, unless it's their "gay bestie," things usually progress to some sort of relationship status. I have one sister, though, that has been best friends with a guy since high school. They both have families now and are still really close, frequently sitting on the phone for hours. I've asked several times if they've ever had anything more than this friendship, and she always says no. She explained that her boyfriend and his long-time girlfriend used to question their friendship, as well, but have both grown to see that they really are just friends.

I truly believe that women and men should be able to have healthy friendships that are just that. It should be like the relationship I described earlier with actual brothers and sisters. My husband believes that men and women can't be friends and says his boys listen to women complaining about their men, just waiting for their chance to make a play. My brothers have very similar beliefs and discourage their significant others from engaging in opposite-sex friendships. I'm not sure if this means that men are the reason these relationships are not so common.

I'm challenging you to be different. Some women don't have big families like I do or close relationships with the males in their families. They don't have men of varying ages to set examples of how men should behave or simply have someone to talk to. And in some instances, it's good for men to have a woman, with no expectations for an intimate relationship and no strings attached, to be able to talk to. Let's all work on having healthy relationships with people who genuinely care about our well-being and who will be honest with us. This is the only way we will start to understand each other more and develop healthier relationships.

Let's face it, your boys do not always give you the best advice. To be honest, there's too much ego and testosterone involved in most conversations, especially if you all have been drinking. And just to play macho, he'll probably advise you to do some mess he'd never have the nerves to do himself. On the other hand, most women will listen, be objective and give you good advice, as well as options, along with possible rewards and consequences. We'll let you know when you're wrong and try to help you to fix your problems. We'll also tell you when she's trippin' and how you should address it.

Even in writing this, I can see what's going to happen. You're going to fall in love with this woman. She listens to you, supports you, calls you on your shit, all the things your woman should be doing. And that's ok to some extent. I love my friends, so it's ok for you to love your female friends. Just understand that all relationships with women that you are close to, outside of your family members, don't have to be ones in which you pursue a romance. They can be genuine relationships, like that of a sister and brother. Respect each other, look out for each other, be there to support one another, and respect the romantic relationships you're involved in. Be a true friend.

Heck, we need it as much as you do. Women like to hear the male perspective on things, and sometimes our spouses or significant others won't be as forthcoming as a man that we are not in that type of relationship with. We may even need some advice, not only about relationship woes but gift options or anything along those lines. I'm lucky, outside of my husband, I have my sons, brothers, cousins, and others to have these necessary conversations with. But what about women that don't have this village of men? They need friends. Strictly platonic relationships between two well-meaning people of the opposite sex that are not looking to be intimate with one another.

Is it possible? Will both people respect this friendship boundary? Are you able to be in the presence of an attractive woman without feeling like you need to come on to her? If she comes on to you, will you politely turn her down and tell her that you're only interested in being her friend? These are the fears that many have, but others' insecurities shouldn't hinder us from doing what we need to do for ourselves. If you know that you are well-intentioned, you should be able to be friends with whomever you choose.

Your Sister,
Wizdom

Doing the Work

Do you have any genuine female friends or women you interact with on a personal level without pursuing them sexually? Yes_____ No_____

If so, how long have you been friends? _____
When and how did you meet? _____
What can you share with your male counterparts about the benefits of this specific relationship? _____
How does it differ from your friendship with your boys? _____

If not, why do you feel you haven't been able to foster this type of relationship? _____
If you're simply not interested, why? _____
Do you feel like you have to pursue all women you interact with that you find attractive? Yes or No
If so, what do you feel is driving those feelings? _____

(Please also share your responses on my Instagram or Facebook. Your perspective is important to me, and I'm sure there are plenty of people that may agree with you. Let's get some healthy conversation started. My QR code is on the last page of this book. Also, please reference the book title and chapter to give the other followers a point of reference. Thank you.)

Chapter 9: Mental Health & Substance Abuse

"For God gave us a spirit not of fear but of power and love and self-control."
2 Timothy 1:7 ESV

Please Read This Before Reading This Chapter
There are two letters in this chapter. The first is a personal letter to someone who is struggling with depression and alcoholism. You may or may not know someone who has these issues, but it doesn't mean that you won't encounter them one day. Please read both letters and try to be sensitive to those that are struggling with mental health issues and substance abuse. I ask that you try to understand their struggle and warn you to be mindful of their mental state, as well. They are not all dangerous, so don't take this the wrong way, but know that many can be, especially when their symptoms are not treated and they're under the influence of drugs or alcohol. Our goal here is to protect them, and get them some help, while protecting ourselves and our communities.

Good morning, Bro!

Woke up with you on my mind. I was thinking about how powerful you are. I also want to make sure you remember that. We all have times when things aren't going how we want, but we have to fight through it. It is sad to watch you struggle with depression and alcoholism. You put on a happy face most days and try to make it seem as though you have it all together. Then as you face challenges, you drink more than your norm, which is already excessive for most. When you drink, you take on a whole different personality. You become extremely aggressive and irrational, and you say and do things that are extremely hurtful to others. Most times, we try to ignore you, but the damage is still being done.

You've been through so much, and you continue to carry yourself as if you don't care whether you see another day or not. Getting drunk in public and getting into fights where you can't even stand up straight to be able to defend yourself is dangerous. Why are you doing this? What is causing you so much pain? What can we do to help you? The entire family is concerned. Sometimes we get to a point where we are really just tired of the shenanigans, but we still love you and wish that you would stop drinking and get your life in order. You are extremely intelligent and charismatic. Everyone loves you and likes being around you until the drinking starts and the unacceptable behavior begins.

Whatever it is that you are running from is not going to be resolved by you getting intoxicated. As a matter of fact, your drinking causes you more trouble due to the conflicts that normally arise from it. When you pass out, you get a moment's rest, and I know you feel terrible the next day. Not only from the physical effects of the alcohol or any altercations but the mental and emotional ones derived from how you've treated people and how they've treated you.

It's time to reclaim control over your life. You know how to eat healthily and take care of your body. You know how to grab hold of your Bible and build up your mind and your spirit. I know the spirit gets weak sometimes, and it gets discouraging. I also know that if you don't give up and fall bait to temptation, you come out stronger in the end. The time is now, my G. I love you and believe in you. I love seeing that handsome, confident, fun, and loving person, and so does everyone else.

Again, without knowing what your issues are, no one will know how to help you. You have to talk to someone who can help you. And I don't mean someone that can just help you out of a jam, but someone who can teach you the skills necessary to live a healthier life. Coping, good decision-making, discipline, and self-control are all things that can improve your life. I know that you want to be happy and at peace. Let's figure out a way to make that your reality.

My little big brother, there is no pressure, but this family needs you to be the man we know you are. I love you. Let go of the past and deal with the present and future. Today is the first day. You can decide how you move going forward. Trust me, everything will fall in line. Take some time for yourself and meditate on it. Ask God for strength and guidance. He's got you! We got you! Love you, dawg! You are the blessed one! Never forget it!

Your Sister,
Wizdom

Dear Brothers,

Growing up in Brooklyn, I witnessed countless people with mental health issues carrying on with their day-to-day life as if everything was fine until it wasn't. Others knew there was an issue, but no one wanted to refer to it as a mental health issue. You would hear statements like, "He's always been that way. He's harmless," or "That's just how she is. Just ignore her." Everyone would just turn their heads and act as though they didn't see what was going on. The shame, embarrassment, fear, or whatever it was, caused these illnesses to go untreated. No one dealt with it, either because they didn't know how to or were in denial. A guy I grew up with suddenly started displaying symptoms of schizophrenia and was actually sent to Jamaica because he was so out of control that his mother could no longer manage him in her home and feared he would get into trouble on the streets. As far as everyone knew, he never saw a doctor either. He was just gone one day, and his younger brother said he had gone to Jamaica. They changed his environment but didn't get him the help he needed.

As a people, we struggle with many demons. It seems as though there's always some battle that we're fighting. I know it gets frustrating at times and can cause a sense of hopelessness. Don't succumb to this. Fight and keep fighting until the issue is resolved. Yes, there are going to be days when you feel like nothing that you're doing is working. Pause, get your bearings (say a prayer, if you need to), reassess, and adjust. Don't get discouraged. Anything worth having will take some work and time. And I'm not just talking about your career and finances, but relationships and other aspects of daily life.

Being honest with yourself and developing grit and good coping skills is very important. An absence of these skills while facing adversity can cause some to lose hope and become depressed or angry. Without proper intervention, some may find other means of dealing with their stressors, such as alcohol and drugs. Some of us self-medicate to numb the pain or relieve our anxiety. However, this does not help to resolve the real issue. You may get a moment of relief from thinking about or dealing with the issue, but this won't make it go away. There are professionals that can help us navigate through these situations. They should be one of our first options, but many times they are not even considered.

I've heard people say that they don't seek help from therapists or life coaches due to the stigmas attached and the fear of people thinking there's something wrong with them or that they're weak. Well, there is something going on, but it doesn't mean that there is something "wrong with you." You're having an issue and you need assistance. There's nothing wrong with admitting that and getting the help that you need in order to move forward productively and successfully. The second part is believing that seeking help is a sign of weakness. What is that? Some type of ego-jabbing nonsense to discourage people from doing what they need to do to help themselves. It's a lie that people buy into and sell to others. I actually look at it as a strength. You are a strong, self-confident person that knows when to ask for help rather than struggling unnecessarily.

Then there's the issue of telling people your business and making matters worse. Guess what? People already know your business. Whether you tell them or someone else does, or they can look at you and tell that something's going on, people know. And the only reason it may feel like the therapist is making matters worse is because they're actually getting to the root of the issue and speaking with you about things you've been avoiding. They're helping you face the issue head-on in order to resolve it versus ignoring it or running away from it. It is a process, and it may not feel good in the beginning, but if you engage appropriately and work through it, you'll be better off in the end.

The minute you start feeling overwhelmed, anxious, confused, defeated, lost, stressed, angry, withdrawn, or depressed, talk to someone, please. You can start with the Father, God. Pray and ask for mercy and healing, mentally, physically, and emotionally. Ask Him to help you out of this dilemma. Ask Him to guide you and give you the wisdom and strength to overcome this situation. You can also find someone that you can trust that you can be vulnerable with and let them know how you're feeling. This person can support you and be your accountability partner, to ensure that you do the things necessary to work through these feelings and get to a more positive, productive place. If you find that you need more help, reach out to a therapist. You can go to your doctor to get a recommendation or just call the number on the back of your insurance card for a referral. If you don't have insurance, you can go to a church or the community health center. There is always an option to find help. These professionals are there for you when you need them, just like you go to a doctor for a cold or a dentist when you have a cavity. There's no difference in seeking help with mental health issues, including alcoholism, when needed. Just a different ailment with a different treatment plan. Resolving either makes you feel better and allows you to focus on other things. You just can't give up on yourself and allow yourself to spiral out of control. Get the help you need as soon as possible.

The mess you were fed as a child about boys not showing emotions or crying and always having to appear to be tough is not true. The people you were interacting with at the time were not properly trained to assist you with working through your feelings. They did not know what to do, so they needed you to just stop. You took a perceived burden from them when you hid your feelings and just sucked it up because they did not know how to help you. They actually did you a great disservice because now you don't know how to properly process your feelings and when you can't hold it in anymore, you spiral out of control. What a mess, huh? Well, guess what? There is still hope. You can still learn the skills necessary to work through your feelings in a productive manner. This does not have to be your life.

This goes for drug abuse, as well. Millions of people self-medicate every day to suppress their pain. It may start out as a casual thing, but we all know when there's a clear dependency. Know that this escape from reality is very temporary. It's not going to solve the problem or make it go away. As soon as you're sober, you'll be right back to where you started, just with less time and money. And if you're one of those that lose control while under the influence, whatever problems you got yourself into while drunk or high are now added on to the troubles you were already dealing with.

STOP! Just STOP for a second. Breathe. Get your bearings. Think about what it is that you need to resolve your issue and who may be able to help you. It may mean that you have to put your pride aside for a moment, but I'm sure this is a better option than drinking yourself to death, putting your life in danger, trying to get so high that you forget your worries, or physically assaulting someone you love or care about. That, to me, is way more negative than asking for help. And if you've already started down this path, choose to make a change today. You can decide to no longer make these choices. You can choose a new plan. Start now. Give yourself a chance at better outcomes and a better life. One where you can walk with dignity and be loved and respected. Because I won't lie to you, these behaviors can cause others around you to give up on you just like you've given up on yourself. And it's not because they don't love you. It's because they don't know what else to do. They're disappointed and tired of begging you to stop being self-destructive. And, to some extent, they need to protect themselves, as well. Start being the strong, respectable man they once knew. One that would fight through the challenges and get stuff done versus giving up on yourself and them.

Again, I'm not saying any of this will be easy. I am saying that it's possible, and the first step is for you to believe the same and believe in yourself enough to try. Just like the rest of us are trying every day. Everyone struggles with something. It may not be the same as your struggle, but it's just as real for the person experiencing it. We all have to pull it together and push through if we want positive outcomes.

Also, remember, whether you want the job or not, you set the example for younger men in your community. Some will mimic your behavior, good and bad. Show them how strong they can be. Show them how to productively move through adversity. Even if you didn't have someone to show you, break the curse and be the change you would have wanted to see. You can do it. You got this! And whether it feels like it or not, you have a village here to support you. We may get tired of your crap sometimes, but if we see you trying to do better, we will be there to support you. This is what we want for you. You must also want it for yourself.

And if you're a friend or family member of someone experiencing these things, try to encourage your loved one to get help. Pray with them and for them, as well. Please don't sit by helplessly and watch them self-destruct and continue to harm themselves or those in their presence. They need you to be strong for them in this time that they are unable to be strong for themselves. We also have an obligation to protect the innocent bystanders who may experience their wrath. Protect them and your loved ones. This person may be unaware of all of the circumstances, which can impact their reaction and cause a very bad ending. The time to act is now!

Your Sister,
Wizdom

If you are in immediate danger or in a situation that is life-threatening, please call 911.

If you or someone you know is struggling with mental health or substance abuse issues, please get some help. Please see the list of agencies below that provide private, confidential help from trusted professionals.

Mental Health America Hotline
Text MHA to 741741 (Available 24/7)

Crisis Text Line
Text CONNECT to 741741 (Available 24/7)

Substance Abuse & Mental Health Service Adm National Helpline
1-800-662-4357 (Available 24 hours/day, 7 days/week)

National Suicide Prevention Lifeline
1-800-273- TALK or 1-800-273-8255 (Available 24/7)
TTY 1-800-799-4889
Live Online Chat @ suicidepreventionlifeline.org

National Alliance for Mental Illness (NAMI)
1-800-950-6264 (Monday – Friday, from 10am to 6pm EST)

National Drug Helpline
1-844–289-0879 (Available 24/7/365)

Doing the Work

Do you have a loss of appetite? Unable to sleep? Are you feeling hopeless and overwhelmed? Do you feel a sense of worthlessness or disappointment with your life or have thoughts of suicide? If so, please get some help. You can overcome these feelings and this moment. Use the resources on the previous page and contact someone that can help you to work through these feelings and the underlying issues.

If you have a family member or friend that has become socially withdrawn, has been sad or irritable for a long period of time, has extremely high or low moods, has excessive fear, worry or anxiety, and/or shows drastic changes in eating or sleeping habits, please help them. Create a safe and calm environment and allow this person to share their feelings without judgment. Avoid confrontation. Just listen, then encourage them to get some help. Resources are available on the previous page.

Think about how you contribute to the lives of those around you. Do you try to be positive and optimistic? Do you motivate people and give them hope?

If the answer is yes, and others that experience your presence agree, thank you. Thank you for spreading positive ripples. Thank you for filling up someone's cup rather than draining it.

If your answer to these questions were "No," please take some time to yourself and try to figure out why. In a world where there is so much disappointment and devastation, we truly need to take better care of one another and try to be more uplifting. Consider the impact you could have if you chose to do things differently. Trust me, making this change isn't just beneficial to those around you. It will help you to feel better and have a more positive outlook, as well. And if you don't have people in your life uplifting you, change your crowd and environment. In the words of Mahatma Gandhi, "Be the change that you want to see."

Chapter 10: Crime & Violence

"Thou shalt not kill. Thou shalt not commit adultery. Thou shalt not steal.
Thou shalt not bear false witness against thy neighbor. Thou shalt not covet
thy neighbor's house, thou shalt not covet thy neighbor's wife, nor his
manservant, nor maidservant, nor his ox, nor his ass, nor anything that is
thy neighbor's."
Exodus 20:13-17 KJV

Please Read This Before Reading This Chapter
This chapter starts with a personal letter to someone with anger issues and
violent tendencies. I decided to share this letter as an example of how
violence doesn't only occur in the streets but can take place in our own
homes. The second letter is a letter to all men, and I am asking for you to
intervene and help to stop the violence in our communities. Whether you
are partaking in it, know someone that is, or if you're not associated with
the violence at all, you can still make a difference. Please read on to see
how.

Dear Brother,

I have to say that I was in disbelief the first time I heard about you putting your hands on a woman. Well, to be more honest, I was absolutely shocked by how gruesome the situation was described. Here I am listening to how the brother that's so loving to me, so helpful, protective, and barely wants me to lift a hand to do anything could possibly do such a thing to another woman. It really broke my heart. So much that I didn't want to believe it.

I'm concerned about where this rage comes from. I'm concerned by the fact that you seem to lose control and get to a place where you're unable to stop yourself from doing something that will cause someone that you love such harm. This is something that I know you're going to regret, which will lead you deeper into despair because of the shame and disappointment you're feeling.

Then when I heard about other occurrences with several different people, I knew that you needed help. This is not the person you used to be. No one makes such a drastic change overnight. Something has been building up inside of you and has now exploded. And now that it's unleashed, you're struggling to control it.

I don't want you to be defined by these things. I want you to know that you can stop, regain control, and respect, and get to a healthier place for yourself and those around you. You don't want people to be afraid of you. You want them to love and respect you. Fear leads to many things, including the need to protect one's own life. The last thing I would want to hear is that someone harmed you while trying to protect themselves. To be honest, they have the right to do so.

And beside me wanting to protect you, I want you to be a better man. I don't want you to be a bully or an abuser to anyone. That's not you, and it's not right. For some reason, it's who you're becoming, but it's not who you are at your core. I've watched you be successful in caring for your family and in your career. Unfortunately, decisions we make may sometimes take us off track, but we are to do everything possible to course correct. You are a strong, intelligent, charismatic young man. You have the time and skills to get back to being the man that you envision for yourself. You have to just want to and be disciplined enough to make it happen. I know that you can do this. I've already witnessed it. You may have to change your environment and the people you surround yourself with, as they clearly have the wrong influence on you, but you can make this happen. If not for yourself, for your children. They deserve to have a healthy dad, mentally and physically, who is engaged in their lives. You know what it feels like to not have that. Don't make this the same for your children. Be the change you wish you experienced.

I don't want to see you going to jail or getting hurt, but that's exactly where you are headed if you don't gain control and refrain from physical violence to resolve conflict. You have to find more constructive ways of resolving issues, and I'm hoping by reading this letter and the one to follow, you may get some help as to how.

I love you and expect much more from you. Love yourself and expect much more, as well. Whatever it is that you need from me to get you going, please let me know. I want to support you in your journey if needed. The time is now. Make a conscious effort to make this change and get it done. Keep your hands to yourself and learn how to manage your feelings when you're disappointed, confused, or upset. Whatever it is that can anger you, identify it and avoid it. Be disciplined and learn how to cope and communicate. These are important steps in your growth as a responsible man. It will be life-changing for you and everyone around you.

(Clapping hands) Come on. Let's get this done. I know that you can. I'll stay tuned, and I'm praying for some good news. I know you want to and can do this. Love you!

Your Sister,
Wizdom

Dear Brothers,

I know that you must be as tired as I am of turning on the news every day to hear that another person has died a senseless death. Or even worse, getting a phone call or seeing on social media that someone you knew was killed. It's just heartbreaking, especially when it's a child that mistakenly got caught in the crossfire. And to make matters worse, the violence isn't just civilian against civilian or race against race. We now have police officers adding to the violence. What are we going to do about this? When are we going to wake up? We have to make this stop. We have to respect life more than we do.

I know that there are times when things happen, and we are filled with so much anger that we think revenge is the answer, but it's not. This starts an endless cycle of paybacks, and at some point, we don't even know who started it. It basically becomes irrelevant after so much bloodshed and grief is bestowed upon us. We have to stop spreading these ripples of pain and start spreading ripples of love and peace. We must take better care of each other.

I believe this starts with the youth, as violent children grow up to be violent adults. We must take better care of our children, instill better values, keep them off the streets, and help them to grow into productive members of society. We have to teach them how to deal with adversity constructively. We have to teach them to use their words and focus on resolutions. We have to make sure they trust us and will share concerns timely so that we can intervene as needed. We must invest more into our children and help them to grow into confident, productive adults with good morals and coping skills. The world has plenty of disappointments, but they are not death sentences. Our children must know how to devise a new plan and keep thriving. We have to give them hope. We need to take care of them and show them love so that they will know how to express these feelings to others, as well.

As adults, we need to monitor their environment, what they hear, see, and think, and set better examples too. If a child is consistently exposed to hostility and violence, they will be prone to this same behavior. Even one traumatic experience can alter their course if not managed properly. This goes for what they see on television, on the internet, at school, in their neighborhoods, and in their own homes. I'm not saying to completely shelter a child by creating an unrealistic expectation of what life is, but I am asking that we correct bad behavior, protect them, and monitor their environment. The opportunities to talk them through certain situations will present themselves, and we need for them to be open and honest, as they can learn through others' experiences and not have to experience it themselves.

Then day by day, as you manage yourself accordingly and have these conversations with your children about life and your experiences, this will provide the building blocks to teach them how to cope and navigate through their feelings and life. We have to put an end to the senseless violence. We should not want our children, whether they're yours biologically or not, to experience the same suffering we have. We should want better for them.

Whatever it is that you can do to end the violence in your community, feel obligated to do it. Start with your own homes and ensure that your family is safe. Make sure they are safe from abusers of all kinds. We should be able to walk outside of our doors and feel safe. Your children should be able to play outside and be safe. The adage, "it takes a village…" still applies today. We should all be looking out for one another and communicating concerns as needed.

If you know that your child is part of a gang and contributing to the violence in your neighborhood, get involved and try to make them stop. If you can't do it on your own, get some help. When I was younger, I saw a lot of young boys get sent away to military school. Of course, at the time, I didn't understand why, but thinking back, the kids were probably out of control, and their parents needed to remove them from their environment and send them to a place to learn better structure and discipline. It may not have to be that drastic but do something. Discourage the negative images and behavior associated with gang members and violent, destructive people. Be very clear about where this behavior gets you, dead or in jail.

When you die, that's it. Your story is over. You don't have a chance to see your family, enjoy your next birthday, right your wrongs, or leave your legacy. You become a statistic, and not by name, just added to the numbers. People may mourn you for a while, but they'll eventually find peace.

If you go to jail, your life as you know it is over, and you become state property. Someone will tell you when to sleep, when to wake up, when to eat, shower, talk, sit, and stand. You'll be living in complete misery and sometimes in very poor conditions. People kill me when they get access to a phone and send out videos like they're having so much fun and hanging with their boys. That's all bull. You'll be away from your family and friends and have no one to support and protect you. You may even be in more danger in there than you were on the streets. Prisoners often feel hopeless, and there are many in there with untreated mental health issues. You won't be able to trust anyone, and you'll always have to watch your back. It's every man for themselves because they all want to get out of there and, most times, will do anything to make that happen. Yep, even snitch. Then, as dysfunctional as it is, you have a few that unfortunately think there's nothing on the outside for them, so as soon as they get out, they do something and go right back in. We call them "jailbirds." I can't imagine the mental state of a person that feels that hopeless. Either way, you're not safe with any of them.

Parents, let your kids know that you want more for them, and they should want more for themselves too. I know it's rough for some youth, depending on the neighborhoods they live in. Most times, they may just be seeking protection and feel that this "brotherhood" can provide that. Or they may just be hanging out with the kids they grew up with and are affiliated that way. If this is so, and the unity is more about friendship and support than drug dealing and violence, then great. However, if there is fighting, stealing, drug dealing, and all the other negative behaviors gangs are known for, this must end. Nothing productive will come of it. The little money you get from stealing and slinging will not change your life but can cost you your life. You may be able to buy a few nice things, but it won't last. And you're destroying the neighborhood. Children are not safe to play in the street, and the grandmas can't walk to the grocery store. You've made it too dangerous for them to be comfortable in their own neighborhood, because you've drawn negative attention from other gangs and the police.

Then we harass, beat, and even kill people simply because they live in different neighborhoods and hang out with different people. Guess what? They have some of the same struggles you do, and they're trying to figure out how to navigate through them, as well. They want to make it out alive and go on to live a prosperous life, just like you do. Stop tearing each other down. Stop making life more difficult for one another. Stop killing each other. If we put that same energy, we are giving now to better our lives and those around us, just imagine how successful we could be. If we learned how to help, love, and support one another, how many more of us would go off to college instead of jail or being murdered? Something must change. We can't just keep doing the same nonsense day in and day out and expect a different outcome. I'm not sure why you think this has to be the way, but it doesn't. Make that decision and do something different, then encourage those around you, especially the younger boys, to be different too. Show them that life has so much more to offer than what they've been hearing and seeing. Help them to have a different experience and perspective.

Our ancestors didn't fight for us to be free to see us behaving like this. Our people have suffered enough and should not have to continue to live in fear and be beaten or killed. This is a slap in the face. Every generation needs to do the best they can to create a better life for the next. Find power in being a part of that legacy instead of further enslaving and torturing your people. Do better.

Let's teach our youth to work for what they want and appreciate what they have. Robbing and stealing are not the way. You can't just take something from someone else just because you want it. If those are the rules, you should be watching your back because another person with those views is coming for you, just like you came for someone else. What type of life is that? Why put yourself in that situation? Work for what you want, just like others have to. Go to school or learn a trade. Find a job or use your skills and talents to start your own business or career. We all have to start from somewhere and understand that we may not get to where we want to be overnight. Appreciate your situation and grow from the process. Enjoy the ride. It may get bumpy at times but stay faithful and put in the work until you get to where you want to be. It takes time, work, and effort to be successful. Stop trying to skip steps. You won't yield the same results. Learn from the examples of those around you.

Stop selling drugs to our mothers, fathers, sister, brothers, and children. You are killing our communities and destroying our families. All drug dealers say, "If they don't buy it from me, they'll buy it from someone else." Guess what? Let them. Let them search for their destruction somewhere else. Maybe they won't be able to get it, and they'll eventually quit. Either way, it won't be on your conscience. Stop being a part of the process and making it so easy for people to self-destruct.

We are all trying to survive. Some of us are even trying to thrive. We can do this without causing harm to ourselves and others. This self-hate that we are spewing has to stop. The time is now. Be a part of the change. Be a leader for positivity. If you truly have influence, use it for positivity. People who have bills to pay and kids to feed need to get a job and find resources to help them take care of their business. There is something for everyone. You just have to find it. It may not be exactly what you want, but it's a start. Just start and figure out what you have to do to get to where you want to be. Then put all of your hustle into that. Fight for what you want, the right way, so you don't have to watch your back or be worried about someone coming to take something away from you, whether it's a criminal or the police.

I've spoken to a lot of people, who have lived crazy lives, and have done things that they regret. They all say they don't really know why they were doing it. It's like a spirit gets a hold of you, and you're at its beck and call for torment and death. You're totally blind to what you're doing and the harm you're causing. A slave to the system. Well, wake up. Shake it off because you can't say sorry for everything. Some things can't be reversed or corrected. Get deep into prayer and ask God to lift this curse up off you and help you to change your path. Ask Him to help you to find another way. Ask that He give you the wisdom and strength to overcome this demon. Ask Him to give those around you mercy and understanding, so they won't hinder your progress but instead support you in your changes.

And when you get this blessing, bless someone else. If we help each other, instead of hating on each other, or having this crab in the barrel mentality, like we all can't be successful, we could accomplish so much more. There are plenty of spoils for everyone. We don't have to fight over any of it. You can have your share, I can have mine, and our brothers and sisters can have there's, and there's still some left for someone else. Correct your mindset and do better for yourself and everyone else around you. You will experience a different world, where you truly feel proud of yourself and what you've accomplished and have pride in who you have become. And don't let the naysayers distract you. Know that they are still lost, and don't allow them to have any bearing on your decision-making. Once your feet are on solid ground, you can help them get it together too. Trust me. I don't care how flashy they look today. You are steps ahead of them. That world is not real and has consequences that only a fool would desire. Be stronger. Be better. I know that you can.

And for the older guys that are out there mixed up in the wrong things and initiating others into a life of crime and violence, have a moment of honesty with yourself. Think about the dreams and aspirations you had that you weren't able to manifest into something real because of the demands of your lifestyle. Think about your regrets and the things you would have done differently if you had the opportunity. Focus your energy on helping other young brothers and sisters avoid those traps. Help to create a different life for them, rather than pulling them into yours. They say, "misery loves company." Let's break that curse. The older generations make sacrifices for the younger generations. Now is your time to do some good. You have the power to save someone else from falling into the life you wish you could escape from. Do it! Speak truth to the youth and encourage them to stay in school, get an education, learn a trade, and make a better life for themselves. And while you're at it, change your life too. Find a way to get out of your current situation and make a change today. We don't run out of opportunities to change our lives until we stop breathing. Lead by example, my brother.

As a community, let's do the best we can to ensure everyone has the resources they need to thrive. We can provide resources like employment, food, shelter, clothing, childcare, safe and structured schools, transportation, healthcare, counseling, and safe havens. It seems pretty basic to me.

I pray that God opens your heart and mind so that you can receive this message as intended. Whether you are the one that needs to change your life or the one that can help someone to change theirs. I pray that you have the strength and wisdom to be successful. Destiny is altered by the daily decisions we make. It's never too late to make a change unless you're taking your last breath. Repent and rebuild.

Your Sister,
Wizdom

If you or someone you know is in immediate danger, was a victim of a crime, or is in a situation that is life-threatening, please call 911.

If you or someone you know is a victim of domestic violence, please seek help immediately by contacting the National Domestic Violence Hotline at:
1-800-799-SAFE or 1-800-799-7233
Text START to 88788
TTY 1-800-787-3224
Local resources can be found at www.hotline.org

Crimes against you are never your fault. Perpetrators may try to make you feel this way to avoid taking accountability or suffering consequences for their behavior. Notify someone you trust and contact the authorities immediately. Love yourself more than you love anyone else.

Doing the Work

There is always a clear distinction between those that contribute to their neighborhoods in a positive way and those that don't. There are people that take pride in their neighborhoods and want to see them flourish, while there are those that pollute them with noise, trash, graffiti, and violence.

How do you positively contribute to your community?

Thank you. Keep up the good work, and encourage others to join in.

If you couldn't think of anything, it's never too late. Think of one thing that you can do and do it. This can range from hosting neighborhood clean-ups to organizing food or coat drives.

I'm challenging families to speak with those family members that you know are contributing to crime and violence and ask them to stop. I know it won't be as simple as asking but figure out what they need to change their life and see how you can help them to accomplish that goal. Do they need a job, a change of environment, or counseling? Let's incorporate some help, devise a plan, and put it into action. Their life depends on it. Help them.

I'm challenging law enforcement to patrol the neighborhoods in the mornings and afternoons when people are going to and from work and school. I'm also challenging law enforcement to clear the corners, storefronts, gas stations, school yards, train stations, and any other areas that we know are breeding grounds for drug dealers, crime, and gang activity. Have more of a presence and discourage loitering and criminal activity. Be sure not to harass innocent people, though. No stereotyping or profiling. The focus is on helping to make the neighborhoods feel safe.

94

Chapter 11: Relationship with The Justice System

"You shall do no injustice in court. You shall not be partial to the poor or defer to the great, but in righteousness shall you judge your neighbor." Leviticus 19:15 ESV

Please Read This Before Reading This Chapter
This chapter has four letters. There's one for my brothers, one for civilians, one for the police, and another for other members of the justice system. In all three, I'm encouraging these individuals to do the right thing. I'm asking my civilian brothers to behave appropriately to avoid negative interactions with the police and asking the others to treat civilians fairly and with dignity and respect. Everyone must do their part to make a positive change.

Dear Brothers,

I'm not even sure of how we've gotten to this place, but I do know that we cannot continue down this road. This senseless violence between civilians and police is insane. We have policemen and women that are in place to maintain order and minimize violence and chaos. They are there for us to call upon in emergencies. Unfortunately, this system has been infiltrated by cowards, racists, and gangsters that have created great injustices amongst our people. Now, we can't tell the good from the bad, and this has created chaos. The number of unjustified killings has grown to such proportions that civilians are now taking matters into their own hands and have waged war against the police. We have good cops that are dying because to those that are angry and grieving, they are all the same. They can't tell the difference and can't take the chance to try because they can end up on the wrong end of the barrel.

What is this world coming to? How can we go on like this? We are afraid to be pulled over. We are afraid for our children to be out on their own. We can't even answer our door to a police officer without being in fear that something may go wrong. "Why are they here?" "What do they want?" "Is that even a real cop?" It's madness! We all have a part in creating the necessary balance. Do your part and expect everyone else too, as well. We are all accountable to one another.

Your Sister,
Wizdom

To My Civilian Brothers,

Please do not put yourselves in any situations where you must interact with the police.

❖ Don't be in the wrong place at the wrong time. If it doesn't feel right, leave. Follow your instincts.

❖ Don't be in public, being loud and vulgar, or doing anything else that's going to attract negative attention. Don't be quick to overreact to situations. Let wisdom and self-control prevail. Analyze the situation and move accordingly. Loud + wild = bait.

❖ Don't do things that you know have a consequence you cannot afford. It is not worth it. Find another way.

❖ Don't let "friends" involve you in things that don't have anything to do with you. If you know, they're up to no good tell them, "No, I can't drop you off there. I'm going in the other direction." "No, I'm not feeling that. I'll catch up with you later." Be straight up so they don't even approach you with the mess again.

❖ Don't drink and drive because you know there's a chance of a DUI or an accident. You don't want to harm yourself or anyone else or go to jail. Plan ahead and catch a ride, an Uber or Lyft.

❖ If you have traffic tickets, pay them. Then you won't have to worry about being pulled over when they run your plates because you know they will. Make sure you register your car on time and have the necessary insurance. You want to be able to drive and handle your business. Make it a priority.

Any situation that can cause you to have an unpleasant interaction with the police, avoid it at any cost.

All that being said, do not run away from them if they are approaching you. You will more than likely get shot. If you do have to interact with the police, follow directions and stay calm. I know we are all about standing up for our rights and defending ourselves. Know when to pull those cards and when to fall back. There is a time and place for everything if you know your stuff ain't right, chill out and try to get through this interaction without any drama. Don't be confrontational or try to run. Provide what they need and be civil.

So many of them are so scared, if not angry, and your temperament can dictate the next chain of events. You do not want to escalate the situation and put yourself in danger. It's not worth it. Live to see another day. File a complaint if you feel they're out of line. It doesn't have to be addressed right there on the spot.

Make eye contact and keep your hands where they can see them. As you're getting what they need, talk them through what you are doing step by step so that they are not alarmed by any of your movements. Be cordial and stay calm. If possible, call someone on FaceTime and let them know where you are and what's happening, as you're being pulled over and before the policeman is at your window. Put the phone on the passenger seat, propped up, so they can see what's going on. Ask them not to speak while you are interacting with the police. They can put their phone on mute. Now you're not alone, and someone else is witnessing the entire incident. If the policeman asks about the phone, just let them know that you were uncomfortable being pulled over and phoned a friend. There's no crime against that, and they should understand. If they don't and begin to get agitated or aggressive, comply with the demands to avoid further escalation. Call your loved one back after the encounter to let them know that you are ok.

I used to get pissed when they pulled me over, like, "What the hell do you want? Why are you stopping me? I'm already running late." I didn't say those words, but that was my attitude. All that got me were hefty tickets, for offenses that I did not commit, like running a stop sign. I tried to fight in court and lost. It's their word against yours, and the judge is going to believe them unless you have substantial evidence. Now, I'm calm and polite and can ride off with a warning if I'm lucky. I've learned how to play the game to avoid unnecessary drama and expenses for myself. Wisdom has overcome my ego.

Most of the time, they're just doing their jobs. Some are just trying to meet their quotas. If your things are in order, it'll be a minimal inconvenience and a slight waste of time. Some of the time, they harass you because of the type of car you're driving, the neighborhood you're in, or some other stereotypical reason. These are the jokers you have to be mindful of and be on your Ps and Qs with. You know the routine. Just follow the process and be able to drive away with the least consequential situation.

Your Sister,
Wizdom

To My Brothers in Blue,

You have taken an oath to protect and serve. Some of you do that with integrity and dignity, and to those, we appreciate you and thank you for your service. Please also help to monitor for the "bad apples" amongst you and protect us from them, as well. They seem to think they've joined a cult of terrorists or a group of gang bangers. It's as though the power they believe they have, has gone to their heads and drove them mad. We do not feel safe with them. We actually know we're not safe with them, as they are working with the criminals in our neighborhoods, killing our children, and creating a hostile environment for us to live in.

Please protect us from them and teach us how to deal with them. Go to the schools and educate the youth on how to interact with the police. Encourage these young people to stay out of trouble and avoid unnecessary interactions with the police. Patrol our neighborhoods and help to reduce and eliminate crime where possible. Deal with us like we are humans. Don't be overly aggressive and quick to judge. Don't adjust how you deal with people based on their race, sex, neighborhood, or culture. Treat us all the same, with dignity and respect, even if it's during an arrest. We need your help and want to be able to exist in unity. We should not be living as adversaries.

Be honest with yourselves, as well. If you know that you are afraid to have a beat, stay in the station and do paperwork or some other tasks. We cannot afford to lose any of our family or friends because you were nervous, drew your weapon, and discharged it without cause. Apologizing cannot right that wrong. Everyone has a position to play, and you need to know what yours is. This is too important to take a chance with. Find your right fit.

Your Sister,
Wizdom

To My Brothers in Other Offices of the Justice System,

This extends to the courthouses, as well. Allow everyone to have fair trials and appropriate representation. Let the evidence speak for itself. Provide fair sentencing. Two people with the same crimes should not be given different sentences. And let the sentence fit the crime. We cannot continue to keep people imprisoned when there are more appropriate options for correcting their behavior, whether it be mental health, substance abuse treatment, or another form of rehabilitation. Let's not just let jail be the only option.

We already know that the prison system is a mess and causes more harm than good, most times. Why is it the first option? We have too many intelligent, talented professionals entering the workforce every day. We need to utilize their skills and be more innovative in terms of reformation for these "criminals." Jail is not always the answer. You'd be surprised by how much better the results are if we take the time to develop better options. I'm not saying people shouldn't be punished for their crimes. I'm just saying we should do a better job of finding out why things happened and how they could have been avoided to ensure they don't happen again. Know what our ultimate goal is and how to get there.

One day we will have a just system where there is trust and understanding. We will be able to reduce crime and save many from unnecessary pain and suffering. When we put our heads together, take the right action, and hold each other accountable in a reasonable and responsible way, things will change for everyone. We just need to speak up when we see wrong, try to stop it, and help those in need so they won't have an excuse for committing crimes. Greed, we can't help. Those people will just have to learn the hard way. However, in terms of mental illness and poverty, we need to get resources for the people in need. We need to help these individuals now, so we won't have to be watching our backs later. It takes a village, and you're a part of it, like it or not.

I'm hoping and praying that there can be peace between the police and civilians. I'm praying that the "bad apples" are identified and relieved of their duties, as policing is not for everyone. I also pray that we can heal the wounds on both sides and gain a sense of understanding and compassion for one another. We need the police to maintain structure. Let's just find the right people and place them in the right positions.

Your Sister,
Wizdom

Doing the Work

We cannot judge a book by its cover. We cannot judge a person based on our thoughts about someone else they share a particular identity with. More directly, not all cops are bad. For those who have a negative perception of police officers, I ask that you take a lighter approach with the next officer you encounter. Instead of assuming the worse, consider the fact that this may be a good cop. Someone who truly wants to help and make a difference. Don't be the one to create the hostility. It all goes well, afterwards, think about how this encounter felt versus previous encounters. What did you do differently, and how did it impact the police officer's behavior towards you?

_____

_____

Share your story and new found knowledge with your friends and family members and encourage them to try, as well.

I challenge law enforcement officers to improve their rapport with the people in the communities they serve. Not only should you actually know the people you are supposed to be protecting, but they should trust you and feel like they can call upon you for help when needed. Think of three people in the community that you can befriend and work with to create a safer environment in the territory you monitor. Examples: High School Principal, Director at the local community center, or popular store owner.

1. Person:_____
   Plan:_____
   Deadline: _____

2. Person:_____
   Plan:_____
   Deadline: _____

3. Person:_____
   Plan:_____
   Deadline: _____

Chapter 12: Mentorship

"Above all, love each other deeply because love covers over a multitude of
sins. Offer hospitality to one another without grumbling. Each of you
should use whatever gift you have received to serve others, as faithful
stewards of God's grace in its various forms."
1 Peter 4:8-10 NIV

Dear Brothers,

We have so many positive men in our communities that are thriving and doing well for themselves and their families. We are proud of you all and applaud the example you are setting. We know that you are busy handling your business and keeping everything together. However, we have a favor to ask. It's not too big, and it won't cost you any money, just a little time and effort. However much time you have to offer. It can be over the phone, via the web, or in person. We just need a little of your time to share some wisdom and offer support to your brothers. We ask that you provide mentorship and guidance to those in need so that they have a chance at achieving the level of success that you have.

So many times, people say, "No one helped me. I had to figure it out by myself." Well, thank God that you were able to do so. However, it doesn't mean that this has to be the same for others. Everyone doesn't have the tools or resources that you did or do. They may need a little boost. It won't take away from your blessing to share some knowledge and provide encouragement. It'll actually add to your deeds and create more blessings.

Wherever there are people that can benefit from your knowledge and experience, please offer them that. Each one teach one, is the saying. If we truly embraced this, what a difference it can be in our overall community. If we were encouraging one another, offering support, lending a helping hand, when able, what a difference it would make. If we have the time to offer and participate in Big Brother programs or create some type of organization on our own that will help young men to stay out of trouble and get guidance to support their path to fulfilling their dreams, what ripples could we spread?

I know sometimes we feel like we don't have enough hours in the day to do the things we need to do for ourselves and our own families. I'm not asking that you do anything that's going to pose a burden on you. I'm simply asking that you think about what you are passionate about and how you can help someone get on or stay on track towards a better situation and future. What do you have to contribute, and how can you implement it? My husband loves basketball, so he's trained kids and coached an AAU basketball team for the last 20 years. I have an uncle that works in IT and hosts computer tech classes with neighborhood kids on the weekends. Both men are sharing their skills to help enhance another's life. They are keeping these kids off the streets and out of trouble during the time they spend with them. During this time that they're together, they're also posing as role models and having an impact on these children's lives.

This type of development doesn't only apply to children, though. You can befriend someone at work and help them to climb the corporate ladder. Provide feedback about executive presence and communication and provide opportunities for exposure. You can befriend a young man in your neighborhood that may not have positive role models and help provide advice and support to keep him on track. Make sure they're going to school, ask how it's going, inquire as to whether he has basic needs to be able to focus on handling his business, etc. There are so many ways that you can touch and enhance someone's life if you try.

And for those needing mentorship, be open when your brother approaches you and tries to share wisdom. Know that it's for your own good, and don't receive it in a negative or insulting way. Acknowledge that they don't have to care, but, for some reason, they do. Know that they see something in you and want to support you. I have had some great mentors in my time. Many of them I now consider my friends. Some were mentoring me before I even knew it and recognized it for what it was. And I needed it. I am grateful for everyone who saw something in me and wanted to help me to become a better person, wife, mother, businesswoman, leader, and now author. I will say, not all of the advice will be easy to digest. You'll need to listen and meditate on it for a while to gain a full understanding. This is why I say to be open and assume they are coming from a good place. Assume positive intent. Hopefully, you will see that your village just got a little bigger.

And don't hesitate to reach out for mentorship, either. If you see someone who is thriving, especially if it's in your area of interest, ask them to mentor you. Ask them for advice on how to get started and what process to follow. Ask if you can contact them if you have questions or hit a roadblock. See these individuals as resources, people that know the way and can guide you. You don't have to try to figure things out on your own. Know that there are best-demonstrated practices for just about everything, and these are the road maps you want to follow. No need to recreate the wheel. Perfect it if you can, but no need to recreate it if there's already a prototype. Then use what you've learned to help someone else. Continue with this positive cycle.

Every man and woman has a role to play in making this a better place, not only for ourselves, but for our children and generations to come. Let's work together and get it done. All of our futures depend on it.

Your Sister,
Wizdom

Doing the Work

Think back to what you just read. Now think about the goals you are trying to achieve at this moment, whether you're a new dad or just started a new role in your career.

Is there anyone that you see that's already thriving in these roles?

Who is this person? _____

What characteristics or traits would you like to gain from interacting with them?_____

Have a conversation with this person, explaining where you are and what you are trying to accomplish. Let them know that you chose to speak with them because you have observed the things you mentioned earlier about their characteristics and traits and would like to be able to reach out to them from time to time as you work towards your goals. Also, let them know that you respect and value their opinion, opening the door for them to share any nuggets they feel with enrich your life and help you to evolve along the path you desire.

I believe this person will be honored to help you. You may be one of a few that has recognized and praised them for their accomplishments. They may also appreciate how humble you are and how serious you are about your own success. Hopefully, you can build a successful mentorship relationship.

For those that want to provide mentorship, opportunities are endless. Think about the areas you thrive in or something that you are passionate about. How can you use this to enhance someone else's life. Do it! Start now.

Chapter 13: Taking Care of Yourself

"The road of life is a disciplined life;
ignore correction, and you're lost for good."
Proverbs 10:17 MSG

Dear Brothers,

I've shared a lot of feelings and thoughts about how you should appropriately care for those around you. I couldn't end there. You won't be able to take care of anyone else if you're not taking care of yourself.

First, I'm going to ask that you build a relationship with God if you haven't already established that connection. Learn, by reading your Bible, what it means to live for God. Then do your best to please Him with your thoughts, words, and actions. Pray, at least once per day, thanking Him for all of the blessings He's given you and asking for wisdom and strength to continue to live a life that is pleasing to Him. Also, ask for protection and mercy for yourself and all of your loved ones and friends.

Secondly, as much as I want you to be the kind of gentleman who treats women with dignity and respect, I also want to make sure that you're treated that way, as well. Surround yourself with people that enrich your life, uplift you, and challenge you to be a better man. Make sure you're treated with dignity and respect, and when that is not the case change your company and environment. Don't allow people to take advantage of you or put you in compromising positions. Your relationships should be mutually beneficial and add value to your life. Know that people that have good intentions for you won't intentionally hurt you or put you in harm's way. And follow your gut. If things don't feel right, it's typically because they're not. Move on.

Also, life can get very busy, and it's really important that you manage your time and not let the day-to-day activities overwhelm you. With the demands of family, work, friends, and all the miscellaneous contributors, you can find yourself running from one place to the next, completely exhausted, and not feeling accomplished or fulfilled at all. Press your breaks and stop. You do not have to live like that.

There are twenty-four hours in the day, and you need to prioritize the things that you need to do, want to do, and the things others expect of you. Create a general schedule to make sure you can organize the time you need for work and play, and also give yourself the eight hours of sleep that you need to maintain a healthy lifestyle. Here's what I suggest, to create a sense of balance in your life and maintain your health.

Your 24 hours should be broken into three equal timeframes:
- 8 hours of sleep
- 8 hours of work
- 8 hours of play

There have been countless studies completed that prove the health benefits of getting eight hours of sleep. This is a simple gift that you can give yourself to ensure you are powered up to accomplish your goals for the day and stay healthy. I hear people say, all of the time, that they know their bodies and they only need 6 hours, and they're good. In reality, they're not. Per WebMD, too little sleep can cause memory problems, feelings of depression, lack motivation, irritability, slower reaction times, a weakened immune system, stronger feelings of pain, a lower sex drive, and bad decision making. Does any of this sound familiar? These are things that will negatively impact your life. This is very similar to people having strokes because their blood pressure is too high, and they said they never felt sick. Medical professionals call these silent killers because you may not feel the effects of the damage that's being caused until it's too late. Get your rest. Even if it's not 8 hours straight, find time in your day to make it up. You'll feel better, and you really need it to function better.

We often hear the saying, "work hard, play hard." I've even adopted it, with the additional rule of giving both equal times. We need to work to be able to pay our bills and take care of our responsibilities. We also have goals that we want to accomplish as we climb the career ladder. With these aspirations, we buy into putting in extra hours to get ahead and reap benefits later in our careers. This works, but it has consequences in other areas of our lives. It spills into the time we need to sleep and "play." That shouldn't be an option. We have to learn to work smarter, not harder. We have to manage our day to ensure we accomplish our goals by staying focused, prioritizing, and simply getting stuff done. It takes organization and planning. We should not have to sacrifice other areas of our lives to be successful in one. We have one life to live and should be able to live our best lives.

Living your best life is fulfilled through what we call our "play" time. Now don't get this wrong. It's not about simply playing and having a good time. When I say play, I'm speaking of all elements of self-care, relaxation, and activities that feed your soul and enrich your life. This can range from taking a shower to enjoying a trip to the beach or a 30-minute workout and a 1-hour therapy session. Whatever you need to do to take care of yourself and your family, mentally, physically, spiritually, and emotionally, is your "play" time. Most of this is enjoyed on your weekends, as many don't work on Saturdays and Sundays. These are our bonus "play" days. I know doing laundry, yard work, and cleaning bathrooms don't really feel like "play" time, but if you incorporate music, get your family members to help, and create the right atmosphere, you'd be surprised by how peaceful it feels, and the memories you can create as you spend this time together. Also, it's important to your hygiene and overall health.

Here's an example of a typical weekday:

10:30p- 6:30a	Sleep	8 hrs of sleep ☐
6:30a-7a	Workout	30 min of play
7a – 8:30a	Shower, Dress, Breakfast	1.5 hours of play
	Get kids ready, fed, & to school	
8:30a-9a	Drive to work (Music)	30 min of play
9a-5:30p	Work, with a 30 min lunch	8 hrs of work ☐
		30 min of play
5:30p-6:30p	Pick up kids and go home	1 hr of play
6:30p- 7:30p	Make dinner, kids do homework	1 hr of play
	and take their bath	
7:30p-8p	Eat Dinner	30 min of play
8p-10:30p	Family time & prep for next day	1.5 hrs of play
	Bedtime routine	8 hrs of play ☐

Now you see why you have the 2 bonus days: Saturday and Sunday. Mondays through Fridays are usually pretty hectic. We need the weekends to exhale, relax, get our houses in order, and prep for the week, to avoid feeling overwhelmed. Some of this may include meal prep and getting your clothing ready for the week. Again, this is all a part of working smarter, not harder. It also means we don't have much time during the week to waste hanging out and being nonproductive. Save that for the weekends.

I know you're still trying to figure out how some of this time is considered "play," so let's talk through some of it. When you pick your kids up from school, they are super excited to see you and want to tell you all about their adventures of the day. Well, the little ones anyway, you might have to do a little digging with your teenagers. Either way, this is precious bonding time where you can learn a little more about your kids' personalities and provide profound advice that will shape who they become as adults. The goal is to make these occurrences meaningful, fun, and relaxing instead of dreaded, stressful tasks. It's all about mindset.

Another plus is having a partner to share these responsibilities with. I reiterate, share these responsibilities with them. Please don't offload this to your wife, as you chill and watch her handle everything. That's not the answer. All of these tasks are only tolerable and maybe even enjoyable when you're not stressed while trying to complete them. We have but so much time in the day. Everyone needs to pull their weight.

This is what work-life balance looks like to me. It's balanced. No one element of your life should occupy more time than the other. We need to give all three areas equal time and effort to thrive. If you're not getting enough sleep, you'll be fatigued and not functioning as your optimal self. If you work too much, you'll sacrifice sleep and family time. If there's too much play and not enough work, you won't be able to properly take care of yourself or your responsibilities, which will cause stress and anxiety. We need balance in all aspects of our lives. Everything in moderation, as excess is typically unhealthy.

You should also use your calendar as a reminder for birthdays, anniversaries, or special events so that you won't get caught slipping. Set everything that's annual on a recurring reminder. Check it every Friday to prepare for the next week. This will give you time to place orders, make reservations, or do whatever you need to do. The calendar on your phone or your Google calendar is perfect for this.

Please make sure you give yourself time to exercise, meditate, or just have quiet time to rest your brain and body every day, as we are typically always in someone's presence and have to engage with others. You need your downtime. No phones or other electronics either. Just you and the peace of the atmosphere around you. Time to clear your mind and reset. If you find this difficult, you know you need to slow down. Your mind should not be racing all of the time. Take a deep breath and give yourself a break.

Don't be afraid to say no, either. Someone is always going to need something from you. If you can help them, and their request is appropriate, then why not? However, if it's going to pose an inconvenience for you or is really just an inappropriate request, say no. It's ok to say, "Sorry. I just don't have the capacity to do that right now." Chances are, they can do it themselves or ask someone else. If you just happen to be the nice guy that seems to never say no, they're going to keep asking. Create boundaries to protect yourself from this form of abuse. It may not be intentional abuse, but a conscious adult should know what appropriate requests and behaviors are. Every situation will be different, and I'm sure you can make your way through the noise. I'm just asking that you don't bring unnecessary stress or burden into your life simply because you are afraid to say no. Think about how many times you've heard it in your life. Are you still breathing? Good. This lets you know that the person making the request will be okay too. But if you feel they won't, go ahead and bless them. Just don't do it at the sacrifice of yourself or your immediate family (wife and kids). The only people who may get a pass are your parents or grandparents, as there are just some people we cannot say no to.

You also need to nourish your body properly. Get your three balanced meals, per day, with the required protein, fiber, fruits, and vegetables. Drink sixty-four ounces of water throughout the day unless otherwise directed by a physician. Take the vitamins and supplements necessary for you to feel healthy and build up your immune system. Don't overindulge in unhealthy foods or beverages. It's fine to treat yourself every now and then but know the limits. For example, some men like to have a beer or drink with their dinner. One per day should not be bad. Let's not turn that one into of three or four. Control these things while you can, as it is more difficult to dig yourself out of a hole than into one.

Lastly, practice good hygiene. I struggled with bringing this up, but it needs to be said. We won't harp on these things, but here are the basics.

- ❖ Bathe, brush your teeth, and wash your face at least daily, especially before leaving the house. If you go to the gym or participate in any activity that makes you sweat, take another shower.
- ❖ Take care of your face. If you have issues with breakouts, find the right facial cleanser for your skin type. There are so many products on the market. Just do a little research and use trial and error until you find the one that clears up your skin and makes it look healthy. If you need help, see a dermatologist.
- ❖ Your mouth is important for many reasons. Take care of your lips, teeth, and gums. Keep your lips moisturized. Brush your teeth and floss. If you have cavities or chipped or missing teeth, see a dentist and get them fixed. This is essential for your physical health so that you can properly nourish your body. And if this helps, women like a man with a nice smile and good breath.
- ❖ If you're smelling yourself, everyone else is too. Then, sometimes you don't, and we do. Find the right deodorant or antiperspirant for you and use it before leaving the house. Some people don't wear deodorant in the house, just to give their bodies a break. If you need it, though, do what you need to do.

❖ Use a lotion or cream to keep your body moisturized. Dry skin is not in style or healthy.

❖ Make sure your clothes are clean, not wrinkled or torn. Whether you go to the dry cleaners, use a steamer, iron, or throw it in the dryer, make sure your clothes are neat, smell fresh, and are wrinkle-free. If it's torn, and can't be fixed, time for the trash. No dirty shoes or dirty shoes laces, either.

❖ Keep your hair clean and groomed. Whether you get a fresh cut, retwist your dreads, or have braids, your hair should be clean and neat. I know that some styles are purposefully messy, that's fine, if it's groomed appropriately. You know what I mean.

❖ Keep your nails filed, fingers and toes. Take care of your feet. If your feet sweat a lot and you have fungus between your toes or under your toenails, get an anti-fungal cream and use it until it clears up. Don't ignore this. It'll only get worse. There's nothing wrong with getting a pedicure every now and again, either. It's better if you have a woman that will do this for you, but if not, just pay for it. Maybe you can make it a date situation with someone you want to treat.

❖ Keep your ears clean too. Using Q-tips after each shower to dry your ear and clean it is a good idea, if you're not pushing anything back into your ear. If you have an issue with build-up, find a safe cleanser and get on a regimen.

❖ If you are a smoker, please wash your hands after smoking and spray air freshener, like Febreze, on your clothes, after each use. Even if it doesn't bother you, the smell is repulsive to those around you that don't smoke. And definitely don't smoke around others. This is bad etiquette. Further, secondhand smoke is bad for everyone's health. We've seen enough commercials about it leading to cancer, heart disease, stroke, lung disease, diabetes, and chronic obstructive pulmonary disease. We want you to be healthy and want you to live a long, fulfilling life. Let's kick this bad habit and have something else to be proud of.

Whew, ok. Hope that was everything. We don't need you to be a "pretty boy," but we do want you to know how to take care of yourself. A little cologne wouldn't hurt either. Don't overdo it, though. Just a few, maybe three, short squirts, and you should be good.

As always, my brother, I'm here for you and want you to be healthy, mentally, physically, spiritually, and emotionally. See a primary care physician, dentist, therapist, and anyone else that will assist you on this path. I want you to be the best that you can possibly be and want you to live your best life. I know this looks very different for everyone, and I'm hoping that some of what I'm sharing can help you get closer to that goal. One step at a time, one day at a time. Don't ever give up. Keep fighting. Make good decisions. Work smarter, not harder. I have faith in you. You can do this!

Your Sister,
Wizdom

Doing the Work

Consider the "balance" we talked about in this chapter (8 hours of sleep, 8 hours of work, and 8 hours of play) and the many tasks you need to complete daily. What would your schedule look like? Fill in the details below.

Time of Day	Activity	Time Spent

Now tally up the time spent based on how we labeled it in the chapter.

Activity Group	Time Spent
Sleep	
Work	
Play	

Do you have the balance we discussed?

If so, great! Stay focused on managing your time and living your best life.

If not, what changes can you make to create some balance? Be realistic, but also be fair to yourself. Slowly make changes until you're able to achieve that balance.

Don't forget to schedule your appointments: a primary care physician annually and a dentist visit every six months. Take care of yourself.

Closing

"A wise man will hear and will increase learning; and a man of
understanding shall attain unto wise counsels."
Proverbs 1:5 KJV

Dear Brothers,

I'm a person that tries to figure out my purpose and fulfill it. Since my early days, I have been told that I had a nurturing spirit, given advice to friends and family, and felt a sense of responsibility to take care of those around me. I'm not perfect, but I know right from wrong, and I know that we can correct bad behavior, no matter how long we've indulged in it. Writing this book may be a part of my purpose. I pray it touches the hearts of many and changes the lives of many. I pray it sparks conversations that lead to positive changes. I pray that someone who needs to hear these words reads them and identifies as a person needing to do better and gets it done. This is not a one-time read. You know what applies to you. Read it as many times as you need to until it clicks. Ask God to continue to feed you knowledge and wisdom and to guide your thoughts, words, and behavior so that you can be a better man today than you were yesterday and for the rest of your life.

I've given you a lot to consider in the chapters preceding this one. I'm hoping that most of it wasn't foreign to you and it's actually in line with how you're currently living your life. I'm not here to say that I know it all. I'm simply sharing with you my life experiences and influences. I've seen a lot of good and bad, and I'm conscious enough to know the difference. I'm also conscious enough to know what paths lead where.

I'm not someone that has to learn by having my own experiences. I can learn and prefer to learn by using my God-given senses (hearing and seeing) and wisdom. We have to know that the generations before us had experiences to teach us so that we can do better and have better outcomes. They walked through the fire for us so that we wouldn't get burned. If we do, we're simply wasting time because we've already seen this movie and know how it ends. The question is, how can we learn from the past and implement practices to design a better future? That's what we are tasked with. Each and every one of us. And we are here to support each other through the journey.

I know that some people don't want to hear what I have to say. They are bothered by my interference. They want to make their own decisions without the input of anyone else, and they know what they are doing. The list can go on and on, and that's fine too. I'll step to the side, and I'll be here to help however I can, if and when they need it. We have to lead our own lives in the ways we see fit. Just know that true wisdom is the ability to differentiate between right and wrong, good and bad, and make the right decisions based on our knowledge and experience. Knowledge is based on facts, not assumptions. So, when you know better, you do better.

Again, I am here for you and only want to see you live a healthy, prosperous, and fulfilling life. These words I shared were to lead you in that direction. I pray that God opens your heart and mind to receive this message in a positive manner and you pull from it what you need to be the best version of yourself. Until next time, my brother, I'm wishing for you many blessings, safety, peace, love, happiness, prosperity, good health, infinite knowledge, and continuous growth. I leave you with this prayer from Psalms 23 KJV:

"The Lord is my shepherd; I shall not want.
He maketh me lie down in green pastures:
he leadeth me beside the still waters.
He restoreth my soul:
he leadeth me in the paths of righteousness for his name's sake.
Yea, though I walk through the valley of the shadow of death, I will fear no evil: for thou art with me; thy rod and thy staff, they comfort me.
Thou preparest a table before me in the presence of my enemies:
thou anointest my head with oil; my cup runneth over.
Surely goodness and mercy shall follow me all the days of my life:
and I will dwell in the house of the Lord forever."

Amen.

Peace, my brothers.
Your Sister,
Wizdom

Doing the Work

Go back through each chapter and review the thoughts that you've documented in the "Doing the Work" sections. Have you done the work that you've committed to?

If yes, great. Thank you for embracing the full experience and doing your part to make a difference. When I began this project, my intention was to truly impact someone's life in a positive way. I knew that much of the commentary wouldn't be easy to hear, but I also knew it was necessary. I could not continue to sit back and watch the dysfunction destroy beautiful lives any longer without trying to help. Please continue on this path and help others to make improvements, as well.

If your answer is no, what is holding you back from taking these steps to hopefully improve your life and the life of those around you? What do you need to get started? Know that you don't have to tackle everything at once. Just take one step at a time. Trust me, you're going to feel so good when you see the fruits of your labor. I promise I would not lead you astray. I truly want to help you improve and enrich your life. Try talking through some of this with someone that you trust. You can also seek support from some of the resources we discussed in the book. You are not alone. There is an entire village waiting to help you. Take that leap of faith.

Thank you to my wonderful husband and children, for the support and encouragement needed to make this dream a reality.

Thank you to my amazing editor, Brittney Smith. I truly appreciate your time, patience and dedication to helping me birth my first book. You've taught me a lot and I look forward to continuing to work with you while completing my series of love letters.

I also want to thank I A.M. Editing, Ink for my awesome book cover. I absolutely love when my vision comes to life. It's as though you took the picture out of my head and put it on paper. Thank you for listening, caring and being patient. I look forward to continuing my journey with you, as well.

Thank you to my focus group, for the time and effort you put in to reading this book and providing useful feedback, to ensure that my message was clear, fair, effective and easy to digest.

Last, but definitely not least, thank you God for giving me the knowledge, understanding and courage to share this personal message with my brothers and sisters. I pray that it is received by the right people and can have a positive impact on their lives and the lives of those around them.

Thank you for reading "Love Letters to My Brothers." I hope you enjoyed it. I tried to keep it as simple and direct as possible. Many of the thoughts shared are basic concepts about what women and society expect from men. Unfortunately, what was the norm in some of the communities we grew up in are not the norms in healthy functioning communities. Let's change this for ourselves and the generations to come. We have the chance to create a better life for ourselves and our children. Let's be the ones that create positive changes. As Mahatma Gandhi said, "Be the change you wish to see in the world."

Stay tuned for "Love Letters to My Sisters" and much more from me. You're going to love it all. I told you at the beginning of the book that I had your back. I'm not only calling out the thing's men need to do better, but I'm also calling out women. Everyone needs to do their part to create a better world for us all to live in, now and in the future. We can do it if we want to, and why shouldn't we? It is time to level up! Now! Today! Don't wait!

Please let me know what you think about this book and provide any requests for future publications. You can reach me on Facebook or Instagram at InfinytWizdom via the QR code below. We are in this together, and I want to make sure that I am providing my audience with what they want and need. All the best.

INFINYTWIZDOM

Made in the USA
Columbia, SC
18 December 2022

74477398R00076